AF255725

"A stunning womanist reading of resistance of Paul's 1 Corinthians. Mitzi J. Smith has brilliantly choreographed and conducted this conversation about an ancient text, its patent dangers and continual reverberations, and sent it soaring with her wise, eloquent, and ethically urgent voice."

—MARGARET M. MITCHELL, distinguished service professor of New Testament and early Christian literature, University of Chicago

"In *Chloe and Her People*, Mitzi Smith's critical engagement with Paul in 1 Corinthians sets the stage for unmitigated freedom for the oppressed seeking answers from the Bible. It is a revelation of how uncritical interpretation and reception of biblical texts can be damaging. Through her Africana, womanist lens, she provides a powerful resource for everyone seeking to impact the world positively through critical life-affirming readings and interpretation of Scripture. This is a must-read!"

—MMAPULA DIANA KEBANEILWE, senior lecturer of biblical studies, University of Botswana

"With *Chloe and Her People*, Mitzi Smith brilliantly shatters the mystifying and opaque glass encasement of one of the consequential leaders in the Corinthian assembly and first-century Christianity. Chloe finally emerges from the dark shadows of Pauline dominance in the Corinthian correspondence to assume her rightful place on the world stage of the first-century Jesus movement as a firebrand to be reckoned with. A spectacular achievement and required reading for serious students of early Christian origins."

—CLARICE J. MARTIN, professor of philosophy and religion, Colgate University

Chloe and Her People

Chloe and Her People

A Womanist Critical Dialogue
with First Corinthians

MITZI J. SMITH

CASCADE *Books* · Eugene, Oregon

CHLOE AND HER PEOPLE
A Womanist Critical Dialogue with First Corinthians

Cascade Books
An Imprint of Wipf and Stock Publishers
199 W. 8th Ave., Suite 3
Eugene, OR 97401

www.wipfandstock.com

PAPERBACK ISBN: 978-1-7252-5327-8
HARDCOVER ISBN: 978-1-7252-5328-5
EBOOK ISBN: 978-1-7252-5329-2

Cataloguing-in-Publication data:

Names: Smith, Mitzi J. [author]

Title: Chloe and her people : a womanist critical dialogue with First Corinthians / Mitzi J. Smith.

Description: Eugene, OR: Cascade Books, 2023 | Includes bibliographical references.

Identifiers: ISBN 978-1-7252-5327-8 (paperback) | ISBN 978-1-7252-5328-5 (hardcover) | ISBN 978-1-7252-5329-2 (ebook)

Subjects: LCSH: Bible.—Corinthians, 1st—Criticism, interpretation, etc. | Womanist theology. | Bible—Feminist criticism. | Bible—Black interpretations. | Women—Religious aspects—Christianity.

Classification: BS2675.52 S65 2023 (paperback) | BS2675.52 (ebook)

04/26/23

Contents

CHAPTER 1

Prologue: Chloe and Her People

Fugitives in Search of Unmitigated Freedom

> "There must be some way to enhance canon
> readings without enshrining them."
>
> Toni Morrison[1]

I began writing this book over three years ago. The COVID-19 pandemic, other writing commitments, the move to Georgia to join another institution, and the personal trauma of my brother's death during the pandemic caused completion of the project to drag on far too long. But an internal voice reminded me of the importance of this project to me and my community, so I did not abandon it. I did shorten the manuscript, electing to creatively, I hope, combine some topics and loosen my grip on others. I endured even when I could not see an end, reminding myself of my original motivation and that I have lingered uncomfortably in this place before, unable to see the light at the end of the tunnel. Toni Morrison wrote that "a writer's life and work are not a gift to [humankind]; they are a necessity."[2] Similarly, as Alice Walker testified in *In Search of Our Mothers' Gardens,* this is the work my soul

---

1. Morrison, *The Source of Self-Regard,* 166.
2. Morrison, *The Source of Self-Regard,* ix.

must have.[3] Over the years Black women and men have contacted me to inquire about womanist readings of 1 Corinthians. I could not name any on those occasions. An African American woman colleague, an ethicist, also asked about womanist readings of NT texts. Womanist biblical scholars have much work to do, she said. I received her remark as a personal and communal challenge.

When I joined the faculty of Columbia Theological Seminary in July 2019, it became necessary for me to teach Greek-based exegesis (I do not like that word "exegesis" because it still implies a dichotomy between so-called eisegesis and exegesis; there is never simply a reading or drawing out of a text). My first year I was asked to teach a Greek-based exegesis course in Galatians, which forced me to look more closely at Paul's writings. While teaching that course, I decided that Paul is a greater problem that I anticipated. It is nothing personal. On far too many occasions, a single critique of Paul has been met with this response: "So what *do* you like about Paul?," attempting to put me on the defensive. Many readers cannot imagine critiquing Paul. Unfortunately, it appears that the apostle Paul has more influence over Christian practice and beliefs than Jesus and the Gospels. Paul remains an authoritative voice on women's agency or lack thereof, sexual ethics, marital relations, and call to ministry, as readers attempt to rescue Paul from himself.

As an undergraduate student in 1981, I struggled with my call to ministry—to what kind of ministry I was called, I did not know. But as I drafted a paper against women's ordination to pastoral ministry for an English literature class, I initially agreed with the Seventh-day Adventist (SDA) church's interpretation of Paul that stated that women should not be ordained to pastoral ministry, since they should not preach publicly. I remember calling my mother to ask what she thought. She said she was taught that a woman should only preach in public if there is no man available or present to preach. That was how she was taught, but that was not how she acted toward my call; she unreservedly supported me and my call, whatever that might look like. She was filled with pride when I had opportunities to preach. I changed my mind about women's ordination and

3. Walker, *In Search of Our Mothers' Gardens*, 241.

rewrote that English paper, arguing that the SDA prophetess Ellen G. White said women can and should preach. Ellen White was my primary source. Next I attempted to interpret Paul in his first-century context, as a non-scholar, to make sense of what Paul wrote. I wanted him to support women's ordination and call to preach. I have evolved from that position. As a biblical scholar, I have turned my attention toward Paul, and we are simply at odds on a number of things. I believe God called me, met me personally, tapped me on the shoulder, before the church or any woman or man affirmed my call. My call is a very intimate personal encounter with the Divine. The apostle Paul was not there, so he has no say in the matter.

In this womanist reading of 1 Corinthians, *Chloe and Her People*, I continue to free myself to see the apostle Paul as the imperfect and fallible man that he was and whose approval I do not need. Paul demonstrates everything from callous oppressive patriarchy to moderation and/or ambivalence toward enslavement, the enslaved, and women. But it seems we, like the women interpreters before us, always retain something of the master's tools while trying to dismantle the master's house and constructing our own tools. For example, Caritas Pirckheimer, a sixteenth-century nun, deployed Paul's writings, particularly 1 Corinthians 7:38 to counter the claims of Lutheran preachers lodged against nuns: Marriage is honorable, but it is even better not to marry.[4] For Emilie Du Chatelet, an eighteenth-century mathematician and physicist, the Bible was problematic; it was filled with inaccuracies. Du Chatelet argued that Jesus was "not divine but was a charlatan who deceived his followers."[5] She suspected the relationship between Jesus and the beloved disciple as "not very honorable."[6] Ironically, she apparently regarded Paul's writings as more authoritative than the Gospels and the Jesus of the Gospels. Du Chatelet felt the Catholic Church sinned by requiring nuns to cut their hair, since Paul taught that the cutting of women's hair was shameful in 1 Corinthians 11:6.

In the nineteenth century, women like Harriet Livermore and Jarena Lee defended Paul's words in 1 Corinthians, arguing that

---

4. Schroeder and Taylor, *Voices Long Silenced*, 91.

5. Schroeder and Taylor, *Voices Long Silenced*, 148.

6. Schroeder and Taylor, *Voices Long Silenced*, 148.

those who use 1 Corinthians 14 and 1 Corinthians 11, respectively, against women's right to preach "misread Paul." This is the position taken in our current context by so-called liberals when fundamentalist and/or far right-leaning white nationalist Christians weaponize Paul's writings (e.g., Rom 13:1) to support their position that citizens should obey governmental authorities, at least those leaders whom they voted for and who support their cause or political agenda. Like Livermore and Lee, the English woman Catherine Mumford Booth (1829–90), co-founder of the Salvation Army, published a pamphlet titled *Female Ministry; or, Woman's Right to Preach the Gospel* (1859) in which she argued that Paul had been misinterpreted in 1 Corinthians 14. Booth believed that the inexcusable weaponization of 1 Corinthians 14:34 mandating that women remain silent in the churches constituted the greatest error of "biblical interpretation of texts related to women"; it negatively impacted the church, contributed to evil in the world, and dishonored God.[7] I argue that Paul can be, and too often is, problematic without being misread.

Paul's letters, especially 1 and 2 Corinthians and Galatians were popular among African Americans who wrote, preached, and lectured in the eighteenth through the twentieth centuries. African Americans' fondness for and use of 1 Corinthians as a resource is even more apparent when we read Lisa Bowens's book *African American Readings of Paul*.[8] For example, the African preacher John Jea (1773–1817) often cites 1 Corinthians in his autobiography. Jea deploys Paul's rhetoric in 1 Corinthians uncritically to describe his own preaching ministry.[9] Bowens asserts that Lemuel Haynes (1753–1833), the first Black American ordained by any religious organization, is an "important early black Pauline exegete."[10] Haynes argues in his reading of 1 Corinthians 7:21 that Paul advocated for freedom for the enslaved whenever freedom was lawfully attainable.[11] Unfortunately, Haynes also asserted that spiri-

---

7. Schroeder and Taylor, *Voices Long Silenced*, 161.

8. Bowens, *African American Readings of Paul*. See also Powery and Sadler, *Genesis of Liberation*.

9. Bowens, *African American Readings of Paul*, 770, 1.

10. Bowens, *African American Readings of Paul*, 49.

11. Bowens, *African American Readings of Paul*, 52.

tual freedom is more significant than material freedom, without denying the importance of the latter.[12] Haynes sounds like the moderate that Paul is regarding enslavement and liberation.[13] As an MDiv student, I too once argued that Paul favored freedom for the enslaved in 1 Corinthians 7:21; perhaps, I needed to view Paul as an ancient abolitionist of sorts.[14] Nineteenth-century Black preaching women like Jarena Lee, one of the first Black women preachers in the AME church, cited Paul to support women's call to preach and did not critique him. Lee asserted that Mary was the first to preach the resurrection of Jesus, and she notes the significance of the resurrection for Christian doctrine and hope, as Paul argued. Yet Lee ignored the exclusion of Mary from Paul's list in 1 Corinthians 15 as one to whom the risen Jesus appeared. Paul only names men.[15] In her 1833 farewell address in Boston, Maria Stewart (1803–79), the first female public lecturer on the subject of politics, expresses her opposition to Paul's teaching that shames a woman who speaks in public (1 Cor 14:34–35). Stewart shames Paul: Jesus the great High Priest did not condemn women (Heb 4:14).[16] Still Stewart could not resist trying to justify or excuse Paul: "Did St. Paul but know of our wrongs and deprivations, I presume he would make no objections to our pleading in public for our rights."[17] Certainly, Paul was not ignorant of the dehumanizing brutality of enslavement for women and men under the Roman empire and the violence of patriarchy.

No doubt a major reason for uncritical acceptance of Paul's testimony is the fact that almost half of the New Testament, as the sacred authoritative writings of the Christian church, is attributed to Paul's authorship and written to early Christ groups or assemblies (churches). Many modern Christian readers view the apostle Paul as God's post-Jesus representative who disseminates objective spiritual advice that transcends time and culture.

---

12. Bowens, *African American Readings of Paul*, 52.

13. Smith and Choi, *Minoritized Women Reading Race and Ethnicity*.

14. Smith, "Slavery and the Early Church."

15. Bowens, *African American Readings of Paul*, 78.

16. Bowens, *African American Readings of Paul*, 139.

17. Bowens, *African American Readings of Paul*, 139.

The African American readers of Scripture in Bowens's book *African American Readings of Paul* overwhelmingly and uncritically embraced Paul and his writings. Pauline writings are treated as a sourcebook in freedom, despite the weaponization of admonishments to the enslaved to obey their masters. While Howard Thurman's grandmother Nancy Ambrose rejected Paul's writings because of their use to support the enslavement of Black peoples, she uncritically salvaged 1 Corinthians 13.

Chloe and Her People offers a womanist's critical reading of Paul's rhetoric in 1 Corinthians. I focus primarily but not exclusively on those texts that I find problematic and/or antithetical to Black people's struggle for unmitigated freedom as fugitives in a land of freedom. For formerly enslaved Black women and men negotiating life and faith in a post-apocalyptic racialized world, freedom is not absolute or free. The womanist readings in *Chloe and Her People* create a dialogue between my contextual analyses of texts in 1 Corinthians chapters 1–4, 7, 11–14 and Africana women's histories, artifacts, voices, traditions, ways of knowing, knowledge production, and contemporary struggles as liberated fugitives striving for unmitigated freedom.

In chapter 2, "Chloe, a Freedwoman in First-Century Corinth, and Frances Watkins Harper's Aunt Chloe," I argue that Chloe was a gifted freedwoman who owned enslaved persons (those who belong to Chloe) and one of the leaders of an assembly named after her. This identification of Chloe is based on Antoinette Clark Wire's reconstruction of the Corinthian women prophets in *The Corinthian Women Prophets*, Paul's rhetoric in 1 Corinthians, knowledge of ancient first-century Corinth as a Roman colony populated with freedpersons, and ancient inscriptions that identify *Chloe* as a name typically given to enslaved females. By placing my reconstruction of Chloe and her people in conversation with Frances Watkins Harper's Aunt Chloe poems, I further reimagine how Corinth's Chloe negotiated life as an enslaved woman and later a freedwoman living in stigmatized flesh.

In chapter 3, "Paul's Rhetorical Construction of Divine and Worldly Epistemologies, the Apollos Threat, and Africana Wholistic Knowledge," I read Paul's rhetorical construction of binary epistemologies (worldly and Divine knowledge and wisdom) through the framework of and in conversation with Black women and men's experiences of wholistic knowledge. I argue that Apollos is Paul's major rival and a challenge to achieving unity under his authority as chief apostle. Historically Black bodies were, and continue to be, contested sites of knowledge, knowledge-production, speech/voice, and wisdom, as are the bodies of Apollos and Chloe. Apollos's body and ministry are also contested space in 1 Corinthians. His reputation among the Corinthian believers and the party that bears his name are significant problems for Paul, as particularly demonstrated in the rhetoric of chapters 1–4. U.S. pro-slavery advocates and anti-slavery abolitionists weaponized the story of Apollos in Acts and Paul's claim of spiritual knowledge to support their causes.

Chapter 4, "Hands Off Our Hair, Paul! Reading Quarely and Transgressively to Shatter the Glass Ceiling Placed on Our Heads," is a womanist reading of 1 Corinthians 11:1–16 through the lens of and in conversation with the historical and recent policing and criminalization of Black people's hairstyles, which transgress and transgender Pauline theo-ideology and dominant whitened expectations. This chapter culminates with poetic protest: "I am the glory of my hair."

Chapter 5, "Paul's Sexual Politics and Black Women's Contested Love: Reclaiming Hope and the Necessity of Self-Love," discusses the sexual politics and ethics that Paul rhetorically constructs and advocates that men and women among the Corinthian believers should embrace and practice. Given the impending crisis that confronts them, Paul's sexual politics and ethics have nothing to do with love, do not insist on marriage, demand self-control in monogamous relationships, and aim to prevent sexual immorality. Five chapters separate the Pauline sexual ethics of chapter 7 and Paul's prescriptive characterization of love in chapter 13 of 1 Corinthians, but the language of God's gift links the two chapters. I create a dialogue between my critical reading of chapters 7 and 13 and Black women and men's historical and contemporary struggles for love. These three remain: faith, hope, and love, but the greatest of these is hope.

CHAPTER 2

Chloe, a Freedwoman in First-Century Corinth,

and Frances Watkins Harper's Aunt Chloe

"Diogenes was free.... It was not because he was born of free parents, for he was not, but because he had cast off all the handles of slavery, and there was no way in which a person could get close and lay hold of him to enslave him. Everything he had was easily loosed, everything was merely tied on.... Therefore, see what he himself says and writes: 'For this reason,' [Epictetus] says, 'you are permitted, O Diogenes, to converse as you please with the king of the Persians and with Archidamus, the king of the Lacedaemonians.' Was it indeed because he was born of free parents? No doubt it was because they were all the children of slaves that the Athenians, and Lacedaemonians, and Corinthians were unable to converse with these monarchs as they pleased but were afraid of them and paid court to them! Why, then, someone asks, are you permitted? 'Because I do not regard my paltry body as my own; because I need nothing; because the law, and nothing else, is everything to me.' This it was which allowed him to be a free man."

Epictetus, a philosopher and freedman
(formerly enslaved of Epaphroditus)[1]

1. Oldfather, *Epictetus*, Book IV.I.151–53, 156–58 (pp. 297, 298). Diogenes

"If Black women were free, it would mean that everyone else would have
to be free since our freedom would necessitate the destruction of all the
systems of oppression."

Barbara Smith[2]

The apostle Paul does not protect the anonymity of the informant
who informed him of the divisions among the believers in Corinth.
People belonging to Chloe, Chloe's people, delivered the information that troubled Paul. Paul reveals nothing further about Chloe, at
least not explicitly. Readers often assume that Chloe and her people
have little vested interest or involvement in what is happening in
Corinth beyond their function as messengers, or perhaps unwitting snitches. Rumor studies show that people only transmit information that is of personal interest to them and, of course, to the
receiver; "negative talk was all too easily generated," more so than
positive talk.[3] We can infer and reimagine more about Chloe's identity, her people, and her interest in the situation in Corinth from
Paul's rhetoric, the sociohistorical context of colonized Corinth
where many freedpersons resided, and Roman enslavement. As
Elisabeth Schüssler Fiorenza argues, scholars must consider the
socio-material reality of enslaved persons in the communities to
which Paul wrote.[4] Building upon Antoinette Clark Wire's book *The
Corinthian Women Prophets*, I reconstruct and reimagine Chloe's
identity in the context of the material lives of freedpersons and the
enslaved and from a womanist hermeneutical perspective that creatively engages the history, experiences, artifacts, voices, and existential reality of Black women and their communities.[5] This chapter
draws upon traditions about enslavement from the ancient Roman

---

or Diogenes the Cynic was a Greek philosopher who was born in Sinope, Turkey,
in the fifth century BCE and died in the early fourth century BCE in Corinth,
Greece.

2. This quote is from the Combahee River Collective Statement on black feminism, originally self-published in 1977 and reprinted in Smith, *Home Girls*, 278.

3. Ripat, "Locating the Grapevine in the Late Republic," 54, 58.

4. Fiorenza, "Slave Wo/Men and Freedom," 124.

5. Wire, *The Corinthian Women*.

and the modern U.S. contexts for constructing and reimagining the identities and socio-material existence of Corinth's Chloe and her people.[6] Further, dialogue is created between the reconstruction of first-century Chloe of ancient Corinth and the fictional freed-woman (formerly enslaved) named Aunt Chloe in Frances Watkins Harper's *Sketches of Southern Life*.[7] Harper's nineteenth-century characterization of Aunt Chloe, which mirrors the real lives of the enslaved and freed, assists in reimagining the lived experiences of Corinth's Chloe, whom I identify as a freedwoman, and her people as enslaved persons that she owns.

This inter(con)textual womanist reading proceeds with a discussion of Wire's reconstruction of the Corinthian women prophets and her hypothesis of Chloe as one of the prophets.[8] Second, I provide a reconstruction of Chloe's identity within the first-century context of Corinth as a Roman colony consisting of a significant population of freedpersons. Further, archaeological evidence, including ancient inscriptions as well as baptismal registries and plantation records for U.S. enslavement, demonstrate that the name "Chloe" was typical slave nomenclature both in the first and nineteenth centuries CE. I propose that ancient slave nomenclature and the substantial freedperson population in Corinth permit us to reasonably imagine Corinth's Chloe as a freedwoman and eponymic community leader who owned enslaved persons (i.e., those who belong to Chloe).[9] Fi-

---

6. This approach to a reconstruction or reimagination of ancient Roman slave life that draws upon modern slave narratives and artifacts is also used by Joshel and Petersen, *The Material Life of Roman Slaves*, and Brooten, "Enslaved Women in Basil of Caesarea's Canonical Letters."

7. Harper, *Sketches of Southern Life*.

8. When I first began using the term "inter(con)textual" in 2017 in my *Womanist Sass and Talk Back* book I was unaware of Tat-Siong Benny Liew's use of the term in a similar manner in his 1999 book *Politics of Parousia: Reading Mark Inter(Con)Textually*. Liew does not generally create a sustained dialogue between the ancient context and text and contemporary texts and contexts throughout a critical reading of a biblical text, but one seems simply to inform the other, as I understand his project.

9. Contra to Osiek and MacDonald (*A Woman's Place*, 108), who mention Lydia (Acts 16) as the only possible freedwoman in the NT; Glancy, *Slavery in Early Christianity*, 49, identifies Chloe as a Christian slaveholder.

nally, the reconstruction Corinth's Chloe is placed in dialogue with Harper's poetic characterization of Aunt Chloe in order to further examine and reimagine the life of the former.

WIRE'S RECONSTRUCTION OF THE CORINTHIAN WOMEN PROPHETS

In her important text *The Corinthian Women Prophets*, Wire argues that Paul's "rights as a free person have been limited by the Christian slave's freedom in Christ and his position as a male is now being lived out in the same world with the Corinthian women prophets. Paul unquestionably sees himself having lost status" to gifted, wise, and noble gentiles, women, enslaved persons, and freedpersons with intersecting identities.[10] Wire's rhetorical reconstruction of the Corinthian women prophets contributes to a more complex view of Paul as a fallible man struggling with, among other things, issues of honor and shame and women's unbridled agency. Paul attempts to convince the Corinthian community of the need to avoid shame (being disorderly) and of how to maintain social respectability.[11] Wire notes that social outcasts, inclusive of women, had no honor in the same sense as freeborn men. However, the (freeborn?) women prophets possess honor because they consider themselves worthy of respect within their communities.[12] We can include the Corinthian women in Paul's "sweeping characterization of this community's verbal, mental, or spiritual wealth"; they are not a "hysterical fringe" but are the prophets that Paul attempts to silence.[13] Possibly, everyone prophesies in the community, and the Corinthian women prophets constitute the "women at large as the spirit moves them to prophesy."[14] Perhaps freedwomen (formerly enslaved women), rather than the enslaved or freeborn women,

---

10. Wire, *The Corinthian Women Prophets*, 67. See Marchal, *After the Corinthian Women Prophets*.

11. Wire, *The Corinthian Women Prophets*, 66.

12. Wire, *The Corinthian Women Prophets*, 65, 119.

13. Wire, *The Corinthian Women Prophets*, 40, 50.

14. Wire, *The Corinthian Women Prophets*, 147, 156.

among the believers would more likely exercise their prophetic and other gifts, as freely as possible, because of their new existential material and spiritual co-freedoms, despite any lingering obligations to their former masters/enslavers who become their patrons in freedom.

Despite her disruptive feminist reconstruction, Wire gives limited attention to enslaved women and even less to freedwomen. Shelly Matthews has noted the inadequate gender binary that functions as the framework of Wire's feminist analysis of Paul's rhetoric in 1 Corinthians, which is particularly evident in Wire's discussion of sexual purity and immorality that does not address the impact of Paul's rhetoric on enslaved persons.[15] While enslaved women are peripheral to Wire's reconstruction of the women prophets, freedwomen receive even less attention.

We should imagine freedwomen among the assemblies of believers or Christ groups and among the women prophets because of the significant presence freedpersons in first-century Corinth. Further, Paul acknowledges the existence of freedpersons in Corinth among the assembly of believers when he, arguably, advises enslaved persons to take advantage of the opportunity to be freed or that enslaved believers remain enslaved if they were enslaved when God called them, depending on how one reads 1 Corinthians 7:21b. Few enslaved persons in any slave society would reject the opportunity to be freed or emancipated. Also, 1 Corinthians contains the only NT occurrence of the Greek noun ἀπελεύθερος, which is a technical term for a freedman (7:22). Manumission/emancipation was often dangled before the enslaved to encourage submission and loyalty. It was neither rare nor guaranteed that enslaved persons would be manumitted under ancient Roman slavery.

What impact would baptism or admittance into the Jesus Christ assemblies or groups have on socially dishonored or

---

15. Matthews, "Hearing Wo/men Prophets," 59. She proposes that it is fitting to use the neologism *wo/men* (coined by Fiorenza, *Rhetoric and Ethic*, ix) when referring to the social agents called the Corinthian prophets, "with [the] slash indicating an expanded notion of the kinds of people included under the sign, across a fluid gender continuum, marked by race and class as well as gender" (47).

stigmatized freedpersons? Did the presence of freedwomen in the assembly of believers result in strife between them and freeborn women, or between freedwomen and men of various social classes (e.g., freed, enslaved, wealthy, and poor freeborn)? If the freedwomen that are among the believers achieved their freedom (freedom is never absolute or without restrictions and violence for the formerly enslaved) prior to baptism, did they expect greater social equality with their freeborn sisters and brothers post baptism, including, perhaps, the dissolution of obligations and deference to their former enslavers who were believers, at least within the assemblies? Did freeborn men insist upon maintaining their social superiority and authority in the assembly of believers or Christ groups?

Wire argues that the social capital that women in the Jesus Christ assembly or group possessed may be reflected in Paul's expectation that the Corinthian women prophets would oppose his theology and ideology. Paul's word was not the final word, as demonstrated by subsequent letters.[16] Clarice Martin asserts that the "rhetoric appearing in Paul's own letters might well have intensified a slave's desire for eyeing the goods of freedom. Declarations that men and women—slaves in particular—had been set free by Christ's crucifixion and resurrection sound formulaic enough to indicate that they might have had broad currency in the movement (Gal 5:13; 1 Cor 6:20; 2 Cor 3:17)."[17]

Questions regarding the social implications of baptism initially occupied Christian and non-Christian enslavers in the U.S. The presence of Africans who practiced Christianity and the prospect of white persons evangelizing non-Christian enslaved persons prompted these questions. Enslavers feared that enslaved Africans would become boastful, discontent, and insist on enjoying the same liberty and rights that free white people exercised. Thus, white enslavers of Africans in the U.S. initially prohibited the evangelization of their enslaved. However, once the missionaries assured enslavers that the enslaved would be catechized to accept their enslavement as divine providence, enslavers consented to the evangelization of

16. Wire, *The Corinthian Women Prophets*, 15, 38.

17. Martin, "The Eyes Have It," 230.

their enslaved. The general opinion among the enslaved was that Christians made the most cruel slave masters.[18]

Again, Wire is certain that Chloe belongs to the Jesus Christ assembly in Corinth and is among the women prophets. Initially, Chloe possessed social capital in the movement. Chloe could also be a widow who owned enslaved persons that act as emissaries, a wife of a nonbelieving spouse, or a daughter of a nonbelieving father.[19] The fact that Paul names Chloe as his informant, against his practice elsewhere (5:1; 11:18; 15:12; normally they are anonymous), may suggest that she is well-known among the Corinthian believers. Paul expects the recipients of his letter to believe him when he writes that Chloe's people informed him about divisions among them, which might be because Chloe is a leader of one of the divided parties.[20]

CHLOE, A LEADER AND FREEDWOMAN IN CORINTH, HAS PEOPLE TOO

Chloe was most likely one of the principal heads or party leaders among the Corinthian believers; she had a proverbial "horse in the race." I agree with Wire that the "real 'split'" in Corinth occurred between "followers of Paul and Apollos."[21] But both Apollos and women like Chloe present serious challenges to Paul's authority, leadership, and influence in Corinth—Apollos because of his eloquent speech, knowledge, wisdom, and consequential impact on the believers who follow him (see chapter 3); Chloe because of her status as an influential, gifted, prophesying and praying freedwoman with people or followers of her own. Of course, Apollos, as an apostle, enjoys greater social and spiritual capital among the Corinthians; he appears to be a more imminent threat to the solidification of Paul's desired status as chief patriarch among the Corinthian believers. In

18. Smith and Jayachitra, *Teaching All Nations.*

19. Wire, *The Corinthian Women Prophets,* 41, 60.

20. See Wire, "1 Corinthians," 160; Wire, *The Corinthian Women Prophets,* 42; Pickett, "Conflicts in Corinth," 120.

21. Wire, "1 Corinthians," 161.

a patriarchal society, it is easier for Paul to dismiss Chloe than to ignore Apollos.

I propose that Paul marginalizes and subjugates women like Chloe and her followers and other prophesying and praying women—married and unmarried, enslaved, freed, freeborn, poor, of noble birth—in his First Letter to the Corinthians because they, like Apollos, threaten Paul's apostolic dominance over a unified assembly of believers, as demonstrated by the formation of eponymous groups among the believers (i.e., "I belong to Apollos"; "I belong to Cephas"; "I belong to Paul"; "I belong to Christ"). Paul names four persons, as if each one has relatively significant numbers of followers in Corinth. It is difficult to believe there were no women leaders among them when we consider the naming of Chloe and her people and Paul's attempts to control the bodies of women who actively pray and prophesy in the assemblies and to subjugate them to men (4:6; cf. 11:2–16; 14:26–40; 15:3–11).[22] Paul likely strategically refrains from explicitly identifying any specific women who are leaders among the Corinthian believers, and Chloe is one of them. The four men that Paul names—Cephas (Peter), Apollos, Jesus Christ, and himself—serve as rhetorical examples for all party heads, which of course should only be male, in Paul's view (11:2–16).[23] Some scholars argue that the slogans "I belong to Christ"

22. In 1 Corinthians 16:19 Paul sends greetings from Aquila and Prisca and the assembly of believers that meets in their home; Paul mentions the husband first perhaps because of his argument in 1 Corinthians that man is the head of a woman (cf. Rom 16:3). He is consistent in his rhetorical presentation of women.

23. Kim, *Christ's Body in Corinth*, 56. Regarding "the Christ party," Kim argues that it seeks to "exercise 'theocratic' power in the community, . . . [and] reinforce hegemonic power based on some combination of birth, region, tradition, and patriarchy. . . . The problem in the community is not a lack of 'unity,' but an overpowering, hegemonic ideology of 'power' over the weak and against the voice of women's freedom and equality . . . [and] lack of respect." The weak(er) members would include the enslaved, freedpersons, and the poor relative to wealthy freeborn men and women. Lawrence Welborn ("On the Discord in Corinth," 87–90, 109) argues, the situation may not have been that material since he views Paul's attempts to eliminate the strife and party divisions by interpreting the situation theologically. Although the Corinthians had doctrinal differences and made claims about divine wisdom and knowledge,

and "I belong to Cephas" are "rhetorical mockery" or parody, as no evidence exists that Cephas (Peter) ever visited Corinth,[24] except, of course, here in Paul's letter. Paul's authentic letters are generally understood to be the most reliable sources for Paul's life and ministry. Even Paul seeks to harvest what he neither planted nor watered in Rome (Rom 1:8–15). Was he successful in garnering a following in Rome prior to his visit? If, on the other hand, Paul names Cephas as an eponymous head of a Christ group in Corinth, but he is not, we cannot put it past Paul to have not named women like Chloe who were actual eponymous leaders in Corinth.

Chloe in Roman Colonized Corinth: A Freedwoman among Freedpersons

I propose that Chloe, a leader of a group that participates in the political and theological divisions in Corinth, was a freedwoman and her people are enslaved persons who act as her representatives or messengers. It was not extraordinary for freedpersons to own enslaved persons.[25] The enslaved persons belonging to Corinth's Chloe served as her agents. The enslaved were often sent on errands to collect rents (e.g., Mark 12:1–12); they were used as emissaries who represented their enslavers. An enslaved person can be both an object owned by another human being and an agent simultaneously.[26] An enslaved man who belonged to the Emperor Tiberius named Hesychus was the enslaved of a freedman. Hesychus, a commercial entrepreneur, made a loan as an agent of the emperor's freedman and of the emperor, making a profit for himself and for both his owner and the emperor.[27]

---

the factions or divisions among the believers in Corinth are political and based on social status. The strife is between the few rich noble people and the poor who have formed political factions engaged in a power struggle.

24. Pickett, "Conflicts in Corinth," 128; Wire, "1 Corinthians," 161.

25. Wilson, "Latin Inscriptions at the Johns Hopkins University," 41; Treggiari, "Libertine Ladies," 49.

26. Lintott, "Freedmen and Slaves in the Light of Legal Documents."

27. Lintott, "Freedmen and Slaves in the Light of Legal Documents," 557.

Perhaps Chloe, as a freedwoman, acted as the intermediary between patrons (e.g., Paul as spiritual patron) and the Corinthian believing community, unofficially. According to rumor studies, freedpersons as "intermediaries between patrons and society" were often used as the conduits for the spread of information from the lower classes to the upper classes.[28] Ripat argues that significant indirect contact occurred between the social classes, which meant that "social inferiors could at times exert a considerable degree of power in their relationships with their superiors."[29] Well-connected freeborn poor people and freedpersons could derive real social influence from their role as political informants transmitting information to elite men or social superiors.[30] Information about a political candidate's popularity (or lack thereof) and chances of success in a society reflects "the mutually recognized fact that information could be manipulated, misrepresented, withheld, or shared with others further magnifying the inversion of the normal balance of power."[31] In Roman society information was not easily accessible, and access to information depended upon one's contacts; the elite classes depended on their own freedmen and clients as well as others for information in a variety of forms.[32] Some elite persons were advised to treat their enslaved well so as to prevent negative talk about them and their households, but encouraged scandalous talk about competitors.[33] Competitors needed information in order to know how to strategize and how to proceed.[34] The apostle Paul's rhetorical strategy in 1 Corinthians is predicated on the information he received from Chloe's people about Apollos (see chapter 3). The most useful informants were those with a proverbial fox in the

28. Ripat, "Locating the Grapevine in the Late Republic," 50.

29. Ripat, "Locating the Grapevine in the Late Republic," 50. Although Ripat's research focuses on the period of the Late Republic (last two centuries BCE), such relationships between freedpersons and patrons likely continued in the early imperial period.

30. Ripat, "Locating the Grapevine in the Late Republic," 51.

31. Ripat, "Locating the Grapevine in the Late Republic," 51.

32. Ripat, "Locating the Grapevine in the Late Republic," 52–53.

33. Ripat, "Locating the Grapevine in the Late Republic," 54.

34. Ripat, "Locating the Grapevine in the Late Republic," 55.

hunt and "members of the non-elite were best able to report the popular climate and thus to help an ambitious man decide what to do next to ensure success."[35] Ripat argues that "social inferiors, and particularly freedmen, might tacitly be recognized as valuable sources of information, but such sources were not generally to be admitted openly—except, perhaps, in the course of campaigning for office" or perhaps for the person vying to become or remain the most authoritative leader of a faith community.[36] It is plausible that freedmen (and women) "fulfilled this function [as political informants] more often than not."[37] The enslaved belonging to Corinth's Chloe performed the task of informants between the community of believers in Corinth and Paul, even perhaps unwittingly against Chloe's best interest as, I propose, a party leader. Formerly enslaved persons and the enslaved were often enlisted to inform to social superiors against their own vested interest or in ways that did not benefit the enslaved or the freedperson.

We can reimagine Chloe as already a quasi-independent, well-connected, gifted freedwoman and slave mistress/enslaver when she joined the Jesus Christ sect. In a slave society like Rome, enslaved persons birthed slaves, but enslaved persons did not own the babies they birthed. Their children belonged to the enslaver/master. But freedpersons could and did own enslaved persons. Freedom is relative, contextual, and never absolute for the formerly enslaved; it is conditional and always precarious in a socially stratified society dominated and defined by and in relation to wealthy freeborn men. As a freedwoman living in a city heavily populated by other freedpersons, Chloe had legally obtained her freedom. Chloe's geographical location or residence and her name assist in reimagining her identity.

Corinth was founded as a Roman colony in 44 BCE and was largely populated with freedpersons (the formerly enslaved). During the first century CE a significant portion of the population may

---

35. Ripat, "Locating the Grapevine in the Late Republic," 56.

36. Ripat, "Locating the Grapevine in the Late Republic," 57.

37. Ripat, "Locating the Grapevine in the Late Republic," 61.

have been descendants of former enslaved persons and freedpersons.[38] The Romans filled colonized Corinth with "the descendants of Roman riffraff and deracinated former slaves . . . [; it] was the epitome of urban society created by empire."[39] Given the long-standing pervasive presence of freedpersons in Corinth and the time that both Apollos and Paul spent preaching the gospel in Corinth, we would expect that the Corinthian faith community consisted of a significant number of freedpersons. Freeborn, enslaved, and freedpersons often lived, worked, and played together or in close proximity of one another, as demonstrated by archaeological remains in Pompeii.[40] Martin states that "the invisibility and marginalization of slaves in the reconstruction of Greek and Roman social history, in which their presence was pervasive, is a paradox par excellence"; the lives of the enslaved, for freeborn Greeks and Romans, was a "hidden transcript" and "slaves were props, the background, the furnishings of the household life, who existed to make daily affairs go smoothly for the free."[41] Paul has made the freedwoman Chloe a literary prop in his rhetoric, but she likely played a more significant role in the Corinthian community of believers.

As previously stated, it was not unusual for freedpersons, like Chloe, to become enslavers (see Petronius's *Satyricon*).[42] In Roman Italy, and likely other places throughout the empire, especially commercial trade cities like Corinth, unskilled replaceable

---

38. Pickett, "Conflicts in Corinth," 120. Slavery was pervasive and slaves could be relatively inexpensive; there was no middle class between the top 1–3 percent wealthy and the poor, and slave ownership was not limited to the wealthiest. First Corinthians implies the presence of slaves; where we find slaves, we will find freedpersons. Possibly, as in Roman Italy, the number of female freedpersons would have been lower than male freedpersons and the age of female slaves at manumission would have been higher given the need to retain them to birth other slaves thereby increasing the human tools of enslavers (Verboven, "The Freedman Economy of Roman Italy," 92).

39. Horsley, "1 Corinthians," 243.

40. Joshel and Petersen, *The Material Life of Roman Slaves*.

41. Martin, "The Eyes Have It," 224.

42. Wilson, "Latin Inscriptions at the Johns Hopkins University," 41; Treggiari, "Libertine Ladies," 49; Kleijwegt, "Deciphering Freedwomen in the Roman Empire," 121.

enslaved persons outnumbered freedpersons, but skilled (or gifted) freedpersons were not easily replaceable.[43] Laura Nasrallah asserts that "numismatic [ancient coinage] evidence indicates that a mix of freedpersons—former slaves—and traders became leaders in Corinth upon the founding of the new colony. . . . Yet the rhetoric about low-status freedpersons may be precisely aimed to discredit the high-status freedpersons who emigrated to Corinth to take advantage of its commercial hub."[44] Corinth's Chloe was likely one of those freedpersons, a gifted and influential leader.

Slave Nomenclature across the Centuries: Corinth's Chloe and "Aunt Chloe"

Formerly enslaved persons or freedpersons often retained the names their enslavers gave them. One way that freeborn men demonstrated dominance and subordination was by exercising their power to name those they conquered, enslaved, and perhaps eventually, if rarely, manumitted. Inscriptional evidence shows that the name Chloe was a common name imposed upon the enslaved, increasing the possibility that the Chloe mentioned in 1 Corinthians 1:11 was once enslaved. The name Chloe, like Onesimus and Phoebe, was a distinctive slave name both for ancient slaves and for Africans enslaved in the modern era in the U.S. Among the Latin inscriptions discovered at Rome outside the Porta Salaria is one that refers to Chloe, a slave employed by a freedman as a *sumptuaria* (a financial regulator of spending and consumption).[45] Another inscription from Rome in the first century CE lists a slave wife named Chloe and her likely enslaved husband.[46] Enslaved persons could marry with the consent of their enslavers. A funerary description of a freedman named Titus Primus contained an "epitaph of his concubine, also a freed slave, named Lucania Benigna. Lucania held a baby girl named Chloe in her arms. The single name designated

43. Verboven, "The Freedman Economy of Roman Italy," 88.

44. Nasrallah, "First Corinthians," 429.

45. Wilson, "Latin Inscriptions at the Johns Hopkins University," 41.

46. Treggiari, "Libertine Ladies," 64.

the child as a slave."[47] An actress called Chloe, a member of the pantomimist troupe of Actius Anicetus, performed in Pompeii and the Herculaneum in the first century CE and was likely enslaved.[48]

The name *Chloe*, like Onesimus and Phoebe, was also a distinctive name given to enslaved persons in the U.S. Modern enslavers often imitated ancient enslavement in diverse ways, including nomenclature. Chloe was also a typical name given to enslaved African women in the U.S. South. We find the name, for example, in plantation records documenting the purchase of slaves;[49] in a baptismal registry of Christ Church Protestant Episcopal Parish in South Carolina (South Carolina Historical Society 1921); and in a slave narrative/fortune-telling guide and census records where Chloe was an enslaved African and later freedwoman.[50] Fictional literature about enslavement in the U.S. also mentions female enslaved characters named "aunt Chloe" (Harriet Beecher Stowe's *Uncle Tom's Cabin*) and "black Chloe" (Lydia Marie Child's *A Romance of the Republic*).[51] A significant section of Frances Watkins Harper's *Sketches of Southern Life* is devoted to "Aunt Chloe's" poetry.[52] Aunt Chloe's story prior to Emancipation can be used to imagine the life of Corinth's Chloe as an enslaved woman before her manumission. Ronnick states that "the motives of masters and the hopes and fears of their slaves were likely not so different in ancient times from those held by eighteenth- and nineteenth-century American slaves and slave holders."[53] The occurrence of the name "Chloe" as a slave name in U.S. enslavement

47. Martin, "The Eyes Have It," 2.

48. Franklin, "Pantomimists at Pompeii," 98. Many actors/actresses and other performers were enslaved persons and freedpersons. Some wealthy Roman citizens kept talented slaves for their own personal entertainment. The emperor Tiberius (14–37 CE) probably possessed enslaved persons and freedpersons who were comedians, mimes, pantomimes, and tradegians (Jory, "Associations of Actors in Rome," 244).

49. Labinjoh, "The Sexual Life of the Oppressed," 395.

50. Gardner, "*The Complete Fortune Teller and Dream Book.*"

51. Tricome, "Dialect and Identity in Harriet Jacob's Autobiography."

52. Harper, *Sketches of Southern Life*; Hill, "'Let Me Make the Songs for the People.'"

53. Ronnick, "'Saintly Souls,'" 177.

and in the first century CE provides an opportunity for imaginative reconstructive dialogue between Harper's Aunt Chloe and Corinth's Chloe, two formerly enslaved freedwomen.

REIMAGINING CORINTH'S CHLOE IN DIALOGUE WITH HARPER'S AUNT CHLOE

The Aunt Chloe poems take readers from that tragic heart-wrenching moment in an enslaved mother's life when her children are ripped away from her to the happiest moment when they are reunited in freedom. An enslaved person's body, sexuality, womb, time, voice/talk, gifts, skills, children bred and birthed, and labor belong to the enslaver from sunup to sundown. Corinth's Chloe like Aunt Chloe lived the dehumanization of enslavement and survived and ultimately experienced emancipation.

As the outsider within, the enslaved saw and heard things. As enslaved women, Corinth's Chloe like Harper's Aunt Chloe knew things that their enslavers did not want them to know, that their enslavers didn't know, and/or they had ways of knowing that their enslavers were unaware of. The *Aunt Chloe* poems begin with Aunt Chloe's fellow plantation slaves informing her, in whispers, that her children have been sold.[54] In her reading of Hagar through the framework of Black women's surrogacy, womanist theologian Delores Williams insisted that God is not always a liberator God, but God promises to be with the enslaved, providing strategies for survival and quality of life.[55]

Enslaved persons whispered about trouble. As noted above, people who engage in rumors do so primarily because of some vested self-interest in the content or people involved, such as the auctioning off of their children to another enslaver. Perhaps, as a formerly enslaved woman, Corinth's Chloe like Aunt Chloe could only start a rumor, so she sent her enslaved messengers to Paul with a whisper about the divisions.

54. Harper, *Sketches of Southern Life*, 3.

55. Williams, *Sisters in the Wilderness*.

The Spirit communicated directly with Aunt Chloe, and perhaps with Chloe of Corinth. Sometime after her conversion, Aunt Chloe heard whispers of a different kind; they were not like the human voices that informed her that her children had been sold, but they foretold of a future reunion: "And something seemed to tell me, / You will see your boys again—And that hope was like a poultice / Spread upon a dreadful pain. / And it often seemed to whisper, / Chloe, trust and never fear; / You'll get justice in the kingdom / If you do not get it here."[56] Aunt Chloe was reunited with her two boys in freedom, just as the Spirit communicated to her.

In freedom, Harper's Aunt Chloe is known as "Missis Chloe Fleet," and no longer as Aunt Chloe. Aunt Chloe is freed when President Lincoln signs the Emancipation Proclamation. But Corinth's Chloe likely received her freedom or was permitted to purchase it after birthing many enslaved babies for her enslavers and because of unwavering loyalty and submission to her enslaver/master regardless of how she was treated.[57] In Ancient Rome, the enslaved could be freed informally (orally before well-known witnesses) or formally, including when the census was taken before the censor, in a proceeding before a magistrate, by last will and testament upon the enslaver's death, or she could be permitted to buy her freedom at the price and on the terms set by the enslaver and with the monies (*peculium*) that the enslaver permitted the enslaved to earn and retain (but such monies always belonged to the enslaver).[58] Chloe of Corinth was likely manumitted (freed) because, from the enslaver's perspective, she was a faithful, loyal, wise, talented, and profitable slave for a good length of time and could be replaced without loss of profit and/or labor.

Harper's Aunt Chloe was likely released with nothing, except the worn shoes on her feet and the ragged soiled clothes on her back in the wake of the Emancipation Proclamation, since not one enslaved person in the U.S. received the promised "forty acres and a mule" when they were set free (those who were freed). But

---

56. Harper, *Sketches of Southern Life*, 3.

57. Smith, "Utility, Fraternity, and Reconciliation," 48–57.

58. Bradley, *Slavery and Roman Society*, 154–73.

eventually Aunt Chloe, would become an independent freedwoman with her own cabin, and she viewed herself as nobility (as did others who knew her), compared to her former life in enslavement: "I got a little cabin / A place to call my own—/ And I felt as independent / As a queen upon her throne."[59] Corinth's Chloe could have been among the freedpersons that Paul considered relatively wise or educated and powerful by human or worldly standards (as slaves go, in the eyes of enslavers and freeborn persons), but she would not have been of noble birth if she was born into enslavement (1 Cor 1:26). Chloe's enslavers probably invested in her training and education while she was enslaved, primarily for the enslavers' long-term financial benefit. "Freedmen bear the fruits of the investments their former masters made in the education and training of their slaves" (e.g., the parable of talents in Matt 25:14–30; Luke 19:11–27).[60] Such investment in Corinth's Chloe would have allowed her to have a skill that enabled her to be independent in freedom. Like Aunt Chloe, Corinth's Chloe felt proud like a queen on her own throne, compared to her previous life in enslavement. Corinth's Chloe, however, might have started life as a freedwoman with some material possessions, the wages (*peculium*) her former enslaver allowed her to keep as she started her new life and so that she would remain useful or valuable to her former enslaver as her patron in freedom. In freedom, Corinth's Chloe is still obligated to perform services (*operae*), sexual or otherwise, to her patron, her former enslaver. In freedom, she owns what Aunt Chloe does not; she owns enslaved people who assist with her continued obligation (*obsequium*) and services to her patron (her former enslaver/master). If as a freedwoman Corinth's Chloe refused to execute her patron's (typically a former enslaver/master) business affairs, she could be found guilty of ingratitude and re-enslaved.[61] The economy of the Roman Empire relied heavily on the skills and services of freedpersons, which of course is due to its heavy dependence on slave labor.[62] The state of

---

59. Harper, *Sketches of Southern Life*, 19.
60. Verboven, "The Freedman Economy of Roman Italy," 94.
61. Verboven, "The Freedman Economy of Roman Italy," 100.
62. Verboven, "The Freedman Economy of Roman Italy," 101.

liminality, between enslavement and mitigated freedom, opens one up to hybridity.[63] The freedperson is always a fugitive striving for unmitigated, absolute freedom. Corinth's Chloe would always be known as the freedwoman of her former enslaver.

In addition to being "queen" of her own household, like Aunt Chloe, Corinth's Chloe was leader of the Christ group or assembly of believers (including the enslaved members of her household) that she convened in her home. Harper's Aunt Chloe helped found and build a church. Uncle Jacob (no biological relation to Aunt Chloe) encouraged the newly freed women and men to build their own "meeting place." They built a church using a share of their meager wages. Uncle Jacob blessed the new structure, praying and speaking with eloquent speech (like Apollos in 1 Corinthians), despite his old age: "His voice rang like a trumpet; / His eyes looked bright and young; / And it seemed a mighty power / Was resting on his tongue."[64] Perhaps, the apostle Paul was Chloe of Corinth's "Uncle Jacob" who encouraged Chloe to convene an assembly in her home and blessed, visited, prayed for, and preached in it. Thus, Corinth's Chloe contributed to the growth of the assembly of believers in Corinth as the church in her home expanded. Perhaps, she also financially supported Paul's ministry in Corinth.

When the Union Army (the American north) won the Civil War and Harper's Aunt Chloe and the other slaves heard that they were free, the slaves "held a jubilee."[65] The newly emancipated men and women "laughed, and danced, and shouted, / And prayed, and sang, and cried, / And we thought dear Uncle Jacob / Would fairly crack his side."[66] Some slaves poured out into the streets, to meet the troops, dancing and marching. Similarly, I imagine that Corinth's Chloe and her people unashamedly and proudly remembered, celebrated, and testified of their liberation when they prayed and prophesied in the assembly.

---

63. Ashcroft et al., *Postcolonial Studies*, 13–14, 145–46.

64. Harper, *Sketches of Southern Life*.

65. Harper, *Sketches of Southern Life*, 11.

66. Harper, *Sketches of Southern Life*, 11.

After emancipation Harper's Aunt Chloe filled her household with her children. Her son Jackey searched for her, and when he found her, he stayed with her.[67] Aunt Chloe insisted that her other son Benny who was in Tennessee come and stay with them too.[68] She boasted about her new life in freedom with her children: "I'm richer now than Mistus, / Because I have got my son; / And Mister Thomas he is dead, / And she's got nary one."[69] In freedom, Aunt Chloe can finally have people who belong to her because they reclaimed each other as kinfolk and can live and interact as kinfolk under the same roof without the threat of being sold away from one another. Chloe of Corinth has people who are enslaved to her, but this does not mean that they are unrelated to her. It is possible that like Aunt Chloe, children that Corinth's Chloe birthed during her enslavement were permitted to live with their mother, even though they belonged to her former enslaver (now patron). I imagine also that Corinth's Chloe, like Harper's Aunt Chloe, rejoices and boasts of her new life in freedom with her people, even if Paul might not approve of their boasting.

As with Harper's Aunt Chloe, Chloe of Corinth's life as a freedwoman was not easy. Aunt Chloe testified that it was downright "rough" but they "weathered through the tempest, / For slavery made us tough."[70] These women had to become tough or resilient to survive the violence and dehumanization of enslavement, but we should not confuse toughness with being invulnerable or invincible or unfeeling. They cried, mourned, suffered from depression, and wore the scars of their enslavement, the visible and hidden wounds and marks. Their enslavement was traumatizing; it scarred their minds, bodies, and spirits. In enslavement and in freedom they experienced unimaginable pain and suffering accompanied by tears, sobbing, and heartache.

In ancient and modern enslavement societies, freed or emancipated persons negotiated and navigated their traumatized lives in

67. Harper, *Sketches of Southern Life*, 20.

68. Harper, *Sketches of Southern Life*, 22.

69. Harper, *Sketches of Southern Life*, 21.

70. Harper, *Sketches of Southern Life*, 11.

stigmatized flesh within systems and structures not built for their long-term survival or flourishing. The thriving of freedpersons was threatening to dominant society. Teresa Ramsby argues that depictions of enslaved persons in Roman literature like Petronius's *Satyrica* demonstrate both the "ridiculousness of the subject matter, [and] the anxieties of the elite social classes who see other groups [like freedpersons] as threatening their control over cultural norms, social customs, and class distinctions."[71] Wealth was a precondition in Corinth for becoming a "local notable . . . if a person was especially rich, even though that person was not of distinguished family, there might still be a chance that he [or she] could make a name for himself [or herself]," as evinced by rich freedmen like Erastus and Babbius Philinus (cf. Rom 16:24).[72] Wealth could earn someone honors and power, but for the freedwoman or freedman the stigma of their former enslavement remained etched in the body.[73] A freedperson could amass wealth and become a powerful contributor and/or patron to a city and still carry the stigma of having been enslaved.[74] Verboven states that "freedmen owed their freedom and sometimes their wealth to their professional talent, but mostly lacked other tokens of social respectability."[75] Despite opportunities to become socially mobile, especially for the enslaved of wealthy and/or noble households and/or those belonging to Caesar's household, enslaved and freedpersons who achieved some material success experienced status dissonance in that they remained socially inferior to freeborn persons. In various ways and to different degrees they were stigmatized and dishonored persons in society.[76] Peterson states that "a servile past marred a freedman's newly acquired citizen status [if she attained citizenship status with manumission] and reinforced [her] marginal position in society."[77]

71. Ramsby, "'Reading' the Freed Slave in the *Cena Trimalchionis*," 67.

72. Chow, "Patronage in Roman Corinth," 114–15.

73. Chow, "Patronage in Roman Corinth," 115.

74. Chow, "Patronage in Roman Corinth," 114.

75. Verboven, "The Freedman Economy of Roman Italy," 92.

76. Smith, "Slavery in the Early Church," 14.

77. Peterson, *The Freedman in Roman Art and Art History*, 124–25, quoted in Ramsby, "'Reading' the Freed Slave in the *Cena Trimalchionis*," 75.

For emancipated persons in the U.S., freedom did not guarantee all the rights and privileges of persons identified as white citizens. Harper's Aunt Chloe and other newly freed slaves faced a successor to Lincoln rumored to have swung the noose of lynching, belonged to the "wicked Ku-Klux Klan," and supported disenfranchisement. Freedom has never been free or absolute, for Harper's Aunt Chloe, Chloe of Corinth, or other freedpersons. None enjoyed the same rights, protection of rights, and privileges that the freeborn dominant citizenry possessed and enjoyed. Rarely was the path from enslavement to freedom and life in freedom unmitigated for the enslaved and freed in ancient society. For example, in 51 CE Emperor Claudius instituted some incentives, one of which targeted freedwomen. In order to qualify for the privileges that freeborn women enjoyed after birthing three children, freedwomen had to birth four children while enslaved. Sometimes the formerly enslaved caught a break. Claudius lifted that requirement, effectively releasing freedwomen from *tutela* or the requirement that freedwomen be under the guardianship of a male relative in financial and legal affairs.[78] This would allow freedwomen the independence to leave any wealth accumulated during their lifetimes as freedpersons to whomever they chose instead of it automatically passing to their patron (former enslaver) upon their death, since at death freedpersons of Latin status reverted back to enslaved status.[79]

The lived reality of freedwomen, as seen through Harper's characterization of Aunt Chloe and Chloe of Corinth's context of ancient enslavement, was contingent, fragile, and subject to oppression, violence, and exploitation. The apostle Paul does not know what it is to live as an enslaved person, a freedperson, or a woman in a patriarchal slave society. When her mistress's ("Mistus") son, Mister Thomas, volunteered to serve in the confederate army, Harper's Aunt Chloe was comforted a little to know that her mistress would know a portion of the sorrow an enslaved woman feels when her children are sold. They were sold when Aunt Chloe's master died, leaving his widow with significant debt; "Mistus's" response was

78. Kleijwegt, "Deciphering Freedwomen in the Roman Empire," 117–18.

79. Kleijwegt, "Deciphering Freedwomen in the Roman Empire," 118.

to sell Aunt Chloe's two boys to another master. Another enslaved mother attempted to console Aunt Chloe: "Oh! Chloe, I knows how you feel, / 'Cause I'se been through it all; / I thought my poor old heart would break, / When master sold my Saul."[80] As with all enslaved mothers separated from their children and other loved ones, Aunt Chloe must suffer in silence and alone: "Then I had a mighty sorrow, / Though I nursed it all alone; But I wasted to a shadow, / and turned to skin and bone."[81] Like Harper's Aunt Chloe, Chloe of Corinth might wish that Paul knew the sorrow she experienced in enslavement and knows in freedom. Chloe would not have Paul to be ignorant of her trauma. Unfortunately, the apostle Paul is either unsympathetic or oblivious to the lived reality of the freedpersons and enslaved among the Corinthian believers. Perhaps, Paul would consider such knowledge as worldly and thus insignificant. In chapter 3, we discuss Paul's rhetorical construction of binary knowledge as either worldly or spiritual in conversation with Black women's wholistic ways of knowing. Harper's Aunt Chloe and Corinth's Chloe know that all knowledge is *embodied* knowing. In 1 Corinthians, embodied knowledge, knowledge production, ways of knowing, and knowledge dissemination are contested.

80. Harper, *Sketches of Southern Life*, 4.
81. Harper, *Sketches of Southern Life*, 4.

CHAPTER 3

Paul's Rhetorical Construction of Divine

and Worldly Epistemologies, the Apollos Threat, and Africana Wholistic Knowledge

"One of [Katie Geneva Cannon's] legacies as a social ethicist is that she worked to bring the moral voices of the marginalized, especially Black women, educated and uneducated, into the academy with the recognition that they deserve recognition as thinkers, themselves producers of knowledge and shapers of moral wisdom."

RENITA WEEMS[1]

"The real architect of the Christian church was not the disreputable, sun-baked Hebrew who gave it his name but the mercilessly fanatical and self-righteous St. Paul."

JAMES BALDWIN[2]

---

1. Weems, "The Biblical Field's Loss Was Womanist Ethics' Gain," 11.

2. Baldwin, *The Fire Next Time*, 44.

"To be a Black female intellectual in this country means, for one thing,
to think, write, and teach under a cloud of suspicion that says you're
not good enough, not serious enough, not smart enough. Forever the
outsider, the interloper, the *other* in a world that centers whiteness and
maleness as the abiding images of inquiry, Black women have rarely had
the luxury to pursue a life of the mind; when they do, they are likely to
wind up working in institutional spaces where they are constantly put
on to justify not just their production of knowledge, but also their very
existence in the discipline."

RENITA WEEMS[3]

During his presidential campaign, former Vice President Joseph
Biden promised to nominate the first Black woman to the U.S. Supreme Court. In February 2022, after a rigorous vetting process,
President Biden nominated D.C. Circuit Court Judge Ketanji Brown
Jackson to replace retiring Supreme Court Justice Stephen Breyer
for whom Jackson clerked and whom she regards as a mentor. Mentors are sources of knowledge, wisdom, and encouragement; they
are models of knowledge production. Of course, Judge Jackson, or
any mentee, was not an empty epistemic slate. Her first mentors
were her parents. Judge Jackson's parents lived the horrors of Jim
and Jane Crow, and they passed on their experiential knowledge,
resilience, and faith to their children. On April 8, 2022, standing on
the South Lawn of the White House, Judge Jackson testified that in
her "family it took just one generation to go from segregation to the
Supreme Court of the nation." When Judge Jackson first accepted
the nomination as U.S. Supreme Court Justice on February 25, 2022,
following protocol she first acknowledged with gratitude President
Biden and Vice President Kamala Harris, and then thanked God for
"delivering me to this point in my professional journey." Judge Jackson declared, "I have come this far by faith!" She did not separate
God or her faith in God from her formal education, career achievements, or her nomination. Judge Jackson's testimony that she has
come thus far by faith means that belief in God and her pursuit of

3. Weems, "The Biblical Field's Loss Was Womanist Ethics' Gain," 5.

academic training and knowledge are organically and/or etiologically interconnected. The knowledge she gained, degrees earned, and her experiences at Harvard College and Harvard Law School (where she also served as editor of the *Harvard Law Review*), were acts of faith in God. As some say, "God was all in it." God was with her at every stage, from her beginning to this crowning moment of her journey in public service. Judge Jackson served for three years as a public defender of ordinary citizens (no Supreme Court Justice has this experiential knowledge), in three federal clerkships, and as a federal circuit court judge. There is, for her, no secular-sacred binary and no Divine versus worldly knowledge.

For many Black religious people, God, faith, and the pursuit of formal education in this racialized world are mutual and wholistically connected. Each inspires and informs the other. Formal education and/or professional training prepares us to fulfill our vocations in this world, the macro-garden of our creativity. Our mothers and grandmothers curated their gardens from the raw and scant materials and spaces at their disposal.[4] We have access to materials, resources, and spaces they lacked and/or that were withheld from them. But like our mothers, grandmothers, and other mothers, we are, as Alice Walker states, "involved in the work [our] souls must have."[5] Judge Jackson's parents were her early role models. She watched her father transition from being a public high school teacher, to a law school student, a lawyer, and finally to serve as a

4. Historically and traditionally, Black people's, and particularly Black women's, epistemologies (ways of or resources for knowing and knowledge production) constitute an organic or wholistic assemblage of faith in God, Divine revelation and inspiration, prayer, community support, resilience and struggles for informal and formal education. Many, but not all, enslaved Africans first learned to read in the context of prohibitions against Black literacy and coexistent violence. White enslavers bombarded enslaved Africans with knowledge constructed for the purpose of making enslaved peoples compliant, loyal, and content with enslavement/dehumanization. Such constructed knowledge relied on biblical texts and interpretations of the biblical texts (e.g., "slaves obey your masters" in the household management codes, and the notion that God, the ultimate Master, watches the enslaved when their earthly masters are absent or do not have the enslaved in eyesight).

5. Walker, *In Search of Our Mothers' Gardens*, 241. Katie Cannon often quoted this phrase, but Walker first wrote it.

county school board attorney. Judge Jackson's mother, also a public high school teacher and principal, supported her husband's pursuit of another degree and career. In cooperation with the Divine, in the world we inhabit, we are compelled, strengthened and resilient in pursuit of education (formal and informal), knowledge, and wisdom, but also always producers of knowledge. Such knowledge, speech, and wisdom are deployed to improve the lives of Black people, communities, and humanity.

Yet, Black women (and men and children) have always experienced violent racialized and gendered pushback, setbacks, and attacks against our character, intellect, and bodies in our pursuit of equality, equity, authority, and power. Influential and powerful white Americans, especially MAGA Republicans, including members of the U.S. Congress and Senate, immediately and publicly expressed opposition to the targeted nomination of Judge Jackson as a Black woman, despite her impeccable and unique qualifications and expertise, as if this country had not for over two hundred years limited, *de jure* and *de facto*, the seats on the U.S. Supreme Court to white men. Fox News host Tucker Carlson brazenly demanded that Judge Jackson produce her LSAT scores, implying they would disqualify her or prove her epistemologically inept. Educated Black women and men are too often presumed and/or constructed as incompetent, unknowledgeable, or lacking expertise. Whiteness relies on the socio-ideological construction of Black inferiority to maintain the ruse of white superiority.[6] Indeed, claims of epistemological inferiority or superiority are deployed when white dominance, privilege, access, power, authority, and identity are threatened. When such racialized accusations of epistemological inferiority are weaponized against Black people, they target Black humanity.

In this chapter, Black people's wholistic ways of knowing, as articulated in the writings of Toni Morrison, Alice Walker, Maria W. Stewart, Frederick Douglass, and George Washington Carver, are placed in conversation with a critical analysis of Paul's

6. One Twitter response to the white lash from @MrAhmednurAli read, "A mediocre white man questioning whether an overqualified Black woman is an appropriate candidate for a job he neither qualifies for nor deserves is the story of any Black woman seeking a position of power."

rhetorical construction of binary epistemologies (i.e., ways of knowing, knowledge sources, knowledge production) in 1 Corinthians. Paul argues that knowledge, speech, and wisdom are either of worldly or Divine origin, but many Africana peoples know differently from the spaces of our mothers', grandmothers', and other mothers' gardens. Paul, however, constructs an absolute distinction and subordinates (and belittles) so-called worldly knowledge and wisdom to God's knowledge and wisdom. But *all* human knowing, speech, and wisdom is human constructed, including Paul's, even when claimed to be inspired or Divine. Yet, some readers uncritically embrace Paul's rhetorically constructed dichotomy between secular (worldly) and sacred (Divine) epistemologies (i.e., ways of knowing, knowledge production and dissemination). Such uncritical acceptance can (and often does) encourage and justify an anti-intellectualism among people of faith and sometimes creates ambivalence about and/or rejection of formal education, especially when daunting insurmountable barriers (based on, e.g., race, ethnicity, social class, gender, sexuality) limit or prevent access to formal education. For the oppressed, anti-intellectualism can function as an emotional and psychological buffer against the shame experienced by lack of access to formal education. Denial of access can occur in various ways, including the school-to-prison pipeline, inadequate elementary, middle, and secondary school preparation, breaking a student's will to learn by convincing him, her, or them of a perceived or manufactured lack of potential or ability to achieve, and more generally speaking, through systemic racism and poverty. Exceptionalism that highlights the few who access and achieve formal and/or higher education, despite poverty and systemic racism, leaves unjust systems, oppressive structures, and poverty unchallenged and intact.

This chapter proceeds with discussion of Paul's rhetorical attempt to unite the Corinthian assemblies under God, Christ, and his own authority. This need arises from the information Paul received from Chloe's people (see chapter 2) about the divisions among the believers that lead to the creation of eponymous assemblies (i.e., some belong to Paul, others belong to Apollos, and a few to Cephas/Peter), and which he deploys as his overall motivation for writing his letter to them. Such divisions threaten or weaken Paul's self-presumed position as sole patriarch of the Corinthian assemblies.

In her essay "God's Language" in *The Source of Self-Regard*, Toni Morrison argues for the interrelatedness of data, information, knowledge, and wisdom.[7] Morrison wrote that "we move from data to information to knowledge and wisdom. And separating one from the other, being able to distinguish among and between them, that is, knowing the limitations and the danger of exercising one without the others, while respecting each category of intelligence, is generally what serious education is about."[8] After receiving the information from Chloe, through her people, Paul responds by rhetorically constructing an theo-ideology of Divine or spiritual knowledge, speech/words, and wisdom over against worldly epistemologies (i.e., ways of knowing, knowledge production, and/or knowledge acquisition, transmission, and deployment). In creating this division between Divine and worldly epistemologies in response to the divisions and/or conflict in Corinth, Paul defines, limits, or circumscribes what counts as spiritual knowledge, speech/words, and wisdom within the assemblies.[9] Morrison writes the following about conflict:

> [It] has a bad reputation only because we have been taught to associate it with winning and losing, with the desperate need to be right, to be alpha. With violence. Conflict is not another word for crisis or for war or for competition. Conflict is a condition of intellectual life, and, I believe, its pleasure. Firing up the mind to engage itself in precisely what the mind is for—it has no other purpose. Just as the body is always struggling to repair itself from its own abuse, to stay alive, so is the mind craving knowledge. When it is not busy trying to know, it is in disrepair.[10]

7. Morrison, *Source of Self-Regard*, 225–350.

8. Morrison, *Source of Self-Regard*, 307.

9. Cardona ("Pauline Epistemology") argues that Paul constructs what he regards as true knowledge, and true knowledge is Divine.

10. Morrison, *Source of Self-Regard*, 262.

For Paul, however, the conflict or divisions are a problem that he seeks to resolve by defining, naming, and controlling what knowledge the Corinthians receive, embrace, and utilize or imitate.

Ironically, despite the binary Paul constructs between Divine and worldly epistemologies, he relies on "worldly" information from Chloe (i.e., rumor) as evidence of the problem of divisions among the Corinthian believers. The Spirit did not tell him so, Chloe's people did. The remedy for the divisions is the creation of another division. Based on the information received from Chloe's people, Paul attempts to unite the Corinthian assembly under God, Christ Jesus/Lord Jesus Christ, and Paul, a trifecta of male headship (see chapter 4)![11] This trifecta does not include Apollos (or Cephas/Peter). I propose that Paul views the eloquent Apollos as the major problem and challenge to achieving unity under God's knowledge and wisdom, as he articulates it. Who benefits from Paul's epistemic logic? Why, Paul does, of course!

Paul's dichotomous view of Divine versus worldly knowledge and wisdom does not reflect Black peoples' divinely inspired struggle to know more than a racialized world desires them to know as they struggle for freedom from oppressive ideologies, systems, structures, and policies. Historically, Black bodies were and remain contested sites of knowledge, knowledge production, speech, and wisdom, as are the bodies of the Corinthian believers and other apostles like Apollos. Apollos's embodied ministry is also contested space in 1 Corinthians.[12] I propose that Apollos's good reputation and following among the Corinthian believers and the party that bears his name is a significant problem for Paul, as particularly demonstrated in the rhetoric of chapters 1–4 of 1 Corinthians.[13] I supplement the characterization of Apollos in 1

11. See Miller, *Corinthian Democracy*. As the Acts of the Apostles shows and as Miller argues, people held assemblies among like-minded believers in their various homes.

12. For readings about Paul as a site of contestation, see Nasrallah and De-Baufre, "Beyond the Heroic Paul," and Concannon, *Profaning Paul*.

13. See Castelli, *Imitating Paul*, on the importance of examining the ideology of Paul's rhetoric in chapters 1–4 of 1 Corinthians. See also Given, *Paul's True Rhetoric*; Wanamaker, "Rhetoric and Power"; Fiorenza, *Paul and*

Corinthians with information about him derived from the Acts of the Apostles. Although Acts was written a little more than half a century after 1 Corinthians, both texts view Apollos as a significant *tour de force* in Corinth. The later dating of Acts does not preclude that any supplemental information it provides that is not found in 1 Corinthians should be presumed to be fabrication as opposed to shared knowledge that the author collected from his eyewitness accounts, even if such information might be subjected to accusations of embellishment in the similar way that Paul's rhetoric could be.[14]

LAYING THE GROUNDWORK FOR DIVINE KNOWLEDGE: UNITING THE CORINTHIAN ASSEMBLIES

First Corinthians 1:1–9 lays the foundation for Paul's response to the information he received from Chloe's people about existing divisions among the Corinthian believers. Here are his credentials: Paul is an apostle called by the will of God to/for the assembly of God located everywhere, not just in Corinth (1:1–2). Paul does not deny the calling and ministry of other apostles, yet he does propose a hierarchy later in the letter using the metaphors of gardening and birthing. He does not share the spotlight well, especially with perceived rivals who threaten (wittingly or unwittingly) his patriarchal (and fictive matriarchal?) authority over believers:[15] Paul declares that "by Christ Jesus through the gospel, I myself birthed you (ἐγὼ ὑμᾶς ἐγέννησα)"; how queer! (1 Cor 4:15; cf. Gal 4:19, Phlm 10).

In addition to identifying the Corinthian believers as the children he birthed, Paul claims Corinth as geopolitical space: he is, in his mind, the chief apostle to the gentiles in the diaspora. As Paula

---

the Politics of Interpretation; Mitchell, *Paul and the Rhetoric of Reconciliation*; Marchal, *The Politics of Heaven*.

14. The author of Acts knew of both Paul's and the Apollos's work among the Corinthians and had his own view of the contested relationship from the various eyewitness narratives he collected and examined.

15. Jodamus ("Gender Ideology and Power in 1 Corinthians," 44) argues that the hierarchy that Paul rhetorically constructs includes the subordination of Timothy.

Fredriksen writes, "Paul's most fundamental sense of himself was as 'apostle to the nations': it was his purpose."[16]

Paul imagines and prescribes the existence of a unified assembly of believers under God and Christ Jesus, to which the Corinthian believers belong (1:2). The assemblage of assemblies that Paul founded constitute a kind of ecosystem that cannot (or should not) survive or thrive without Paul's authority and leadership, adherence to the gospel as he preached it or his interpretation of it, and his teachings, which often emerge and evolve in response to each community's communicated or perceived needs and/or problems. In the gospel Paul preached, God, through grace, has made the Corinthian believers rich, in every way, in every speech/word/matter (λόγος) and in every knowledge (γνώσει) in Christ Jesus (1:5). They lack no gift (1:7; see also 2:14; 4:8), including the word of knowledge, which is listed among the spiritual gifts (12:8). Yet, knowledge and speech are contested sites of struggle and power: Paul argues that the Corinthians should all speak or say the same thing or in the same way (1:10). Presently, they are all saying different things—some belong to Cephas; others belong to Apollos; some to Paul, and others to Christ (1:12).

Every so often a student asks me this question: "Dr. Smith, don't you think we should all believe the same thing?" They mean not only believe the same things but articulate those beliefs in the same way. My response is always an unequivocal "no." Whom or what differences and human agency would we have to deny or silence? What sameness would we insist upon? Whom would we choose to believe and how would we decide? To whom would we give the power to decide? Which denomination or institution would we give the power to decide? Should we give up our agency as individuals to interpret differently and outside the theo-ideological and hermeneutical lines that would be drawn for us by those to whom we relinquish power or who seize power? And what happens when someone decides they believe differently and articulates that difference? Should they be threatened with violence, ostracized, demonized, stalked, and abused or sentenced to death?

16. Fredriksen, *Paul: The Pagans' Apostle*, 136.

Again, Paul knows about the differences and divisions among the Corinthian believers because Chloe's enslaved people informed him. He takes it upon himself to eliminate or control those differences by (re)defining, ordering or ranking, and regulating speech, knowledge, and wisdom. Paul asserts that the Corinthian believers should be completely united in the same mind and of one opinion. When an opinion is insisted upon as the only legitimate one, all other beliefs can be othered and subordinated.

INFORMATION FROM CHLOE: PAUL'S SOURCE FOR KNOWLEDGE OF DIVISIONS IN CORINTH

At 1 Corinthians 1:11 Paul identifies a rumor or report that he received from the freedwoman Chloe's enslaved messengers (see chapter 2) as the source of his knowledge of divisions among the believers. The content of the rumor is either a claim that each group has supposedly articulated or it is the assessment of Chloe's people (or Chloe via her people): I am of Paul; I am of Apollos; I am of Cephas; I am of Christ (1:12). The rumor—what Paul heard from Chloe's people—became the primary, and perhaps only, source of information upon which Paul relied for his own understanding and judgment of the situation in Corinth. We have only what Paul shares and claims was shared with him. We have no idea whether the eponymous parties Paul names (i.e., belonging to Paul, Apollos, Cephas/Peter, and Christ) constitute the complete list; we do know that the list of those to whom Paul claims the resurrected Jesus appeared women are omitted (15:1–11). In chapter 2, I have proposed that Paul likely omitted Chloe's name as a leader; Chloe, a freedwoman and leader in Corinth had people too. Paul expects the Corinthians to take him at his word, which is based on the words of other humans. The very basis of Paul's letter(s) is founded on human rumor or orally transmitted information, on what was made known (Greek: ἐδηλώθη) to him by other humans. The rumor (of group divisions primarily headed by other apostles) is the impetus for the rhetorical construction of a binary between worldly and Divine speech/words, knowledge, and wisdom.

The identification of disparate assemblies associated with the names of other charismatic apostles poses a problem for Paul. Regardless, for Paul the different assemblies create a fracture that he cannot abide. Paul always presents the names of the heads of the other parties in the same order, beginning with his own name, Apollos is second, Cephas is third; and Christ is last (1:12; 3:21–22).[17] This strategic ordering already shows how Paul perceives himself, and wants his readers to view him, in relation to the other *living* men in the list; Christ is definitely not his competition in the same way that Apollos is. Paul is sending a not-so-subliminal visual message, in black ink, that he is first or chief and most significant among the party leaders. But Apollos is a problematic significant contender. Knox argues that Paul cannot "tolerate easily [any segment of the Corinthians] feeling a superior loyalty to any other human leader."[18]

Apollos's influence in Corinth was likely equal to, if not more impactful, than Paul's, despite perhaps having spent less time preaching there. Some Corinthian believers may have attached themselves to the apostle who both preached the gospel to them *and* baptized them. This may be why Paul attempts to diminish the importance of knowing who baptized them. Paul claims that he baptized no one, except, of course, Crispus and Gaius, which is nothing to celebrate and gains no one any points (1:13–14; cf. Acts 18:1–11). And by the way, Paul also baptized the household of Stephanas. Beyond those households, he keeps no tally (1:16), and neither should anyone else. We can infer from Paul's assertion that he likely baptized fewer Corinthian believers than Apollos. Apollos baptized more disciples than Paul, and they are saying, "I belong to Apollos" (1:14). Paul has challenged the importance of baptism as a basis for loyalty or submission to any one apostle or to his or her teachings. Paul asserts that Christ did not send him to baptize; on the contrary (ἀλλά) Paul was commissioned to preach the gospel,

17. Smit, "What Is Apollos? What Is Paul?" First Corinthians 1:10—4:21 constitutes "a well-ordered, closely-connected and strategically conceived unity," and it is a defense or apology directed at Apollos's people (those who belong to Apollos).

18. Knox, *Chapters in a Life of Paul*, 80.

but not by wisdom of speech (1:17).[19] The content and preaching of the gospel is also epistemologically contested speech and activity in 1 Corinthians.

CONTESTED SPEECH AND KNOWLEDGE: RHETORICAL CONSTRUCTION OF DIVINE EPISTEMOLOGIES

Paul argues that the word (ὁ λόγος) about the cross is foolishness to the perishing, but the same word is the power of God to those being saved (1:18). Verse 1:18 introduces the first occurrence of σοφία (wisdom) in the letter, and it permits Paul to introduce its antithesis, foolishness (μωρία).[20] He declares that if the believers think they are wise, they must become foolish (3:18). Paul attempts to diminish any eloquence or wisdom that might be attributed to Apollos thus further mitigating his reputation among his adherents. Those who "belong to Apollos" are rendering Christ's crucifixion impotent. He also reduces Apollos's preaching to eloquent wisdom, removing it from the category of gospel. Paul names and subordinates so-called worldly wisdom to God's wisdom. Ker argues that Paul engages in a "re-interpretation of 'wisdom' before re-introducing the issue of his work alongside that of Apollos."[21] Who determines the content of God's wisdom? Who marks the boundaries between God's wisdom and human wisdom? Why, Paul does! I argue that the binary Paul creates between God's wisdom and the world's wisdom is directed primarily at Apollos and "those who belong to Apollos." Paul places education or erudition and knowledge that one achieves in the world in opposition to his own sacralized teachings, which are also human-constructed but defined and named as God's wisdom.

19. Some ancient manuscripts read "not by wisdom of words."

20. Smit ("'What Is Apollos?,'" 243) argues that "what sets 1 Cor. 1:18–19 apart is that οἱ ἀπολλυμένοι is elucidated by means of the quotation from Scripture beginning with ἀπολλῶ, a form which is almost identical to the name Apollos as mentioned by Paul in 1:12." Smit observes in 1:18–19 allusions to Apollos's adherents ("Apollinists").

21. Ker, "Paul and Apollos," 76.

Ben Witherington asserts that Paul proposes a "counter-order wisdom."[22]

Paul is commissioned to preach so that the cross of Christ or Christ's crucifixion should not be emptied or impotent. Wisdom of speech/word or eloquent or wise speech (as characterized by the world's standards) threatens and renders impotent the message of Christ's cross or crucifixion. Why is the gospel of Christ's crucifixion so vulnerable, in Paul's view? Is it because gospel is itself human testimony, and thus susceptible to human critique? Is it because the contents of that testimony about God's crucified Messiah carries its own precarity or instability since crucifixion was reserved for the criminalized and/or the enslaved?[23] But eloquence of speech and wisdom are often associated with the elite. Paul himself was not void of social status and formal training/education (Gal 1:13–18). One cannot separate oneself from one's cultural or educational formation like removing an old coat. If Paul were interested in the life of the historical Jesus, would he consider Jesus an eloquent speaker who was wise by human standards?[24] When Paul preached in Corinth, he claimed to have been an uneducated man devoid of eloquent speech and determined to know nothing except Christ crucified (2:2; cf. 1:16). Does Paul mean that he choose not to utilize any of his formal training when he preached the gospel, if that is possible? Or is Paul saying that he suspended all rational thinking in order to believe in Jesus as the Christ? To what extent can humans separate themselves from the knowledge and wisdom that has shaped and transformed our thinking, language, speech, and behaviors? Paul asserts that he did not come to the Corinthians with bold speech or wise proclamations but in weakness, fear, and trembling (2:1, 3).[25]

---

22. Witherington, *Conflict and Community in Corinth*, 97.

23. See Reaves et al., *When Did We See You Naked?*

24. The Gospel of Luke states that "Jesus increased in wisdom and in years, and in divine and human favor" (NRSV 2:52; cf. 2:40). It does not speak of two types of wisdom.

25. Guy ("Wasting Time at the End of the World," 67) argues that Paul's "simultaneous claims of maturity and abjection destabilize the metaphor that Paul is constructing."

Paul regularly deploys the Greek intensive adversative conjunction ἀλλά (but/on the contrary) to create binaries that distinguish himself from Apollos (and Cephas) (e.g., 2:12, 45; 4:20). Using the strong adversative conjunction ἀλλά (on the contrary), Paul rhetorically constructs an absolute binary that permits him to distinguish between the speech of others and his own, with the Spirit being the source of the latter (2:4–5). The Spirit guaranteed that their faith would not derive from human wisdom but from God's power. At 4:20, Paul again utilizes the strong adversative conjunction (ἀλλά) to depict the absolute distance and dichotomy between human speech/words, knowledge, and wisdom and the spiritual or Divine. In asserting that God's kingdom (ἡ Βασιλεία τοῦ θεοῦ) is not by speech/word (ἐν λόγῳ) but (ἀλλά) by power (δυνάμει), Paul, ironically, uses the language of empire (i.e., kingdoms are colonizing and enslaving powers) to diminish those he regards as exercising worldly knowledge and wisdom (4:20). Yet, it is generally not the weak that access the literacy displayed in Paul's letters. Paul uses the master's tools to dismantle the emperor's house of knowledge.[26]

Who decides what constitutes a demonstration of the Spirit? Why, Paul does! Paul argues that God's Spirit is the arbiter who distinguishes between the things of God and of the world. Only the Spirit knows the deep things of God, in the same way that the human spirit knows the human (2:10–12). "We," Paul asserts, have not received the spirit of the world but (ἀλλά) of God so that we might recognize the gifts we received from God" (2:12). The evidence that the Corinthians received God's Spirit is their reception of Paul's words (2:14; cf. 2:1–4), for "we" speak not by words taught by humans but (ἀλλά) by the Spirit's teachings, comparing spiritual things with spiritual (2:12). It is not left up to each person to determine, even in community, what constitutes spiritual things; but the authority to determine what is considered spiritual resides with the person to whom they grant authority to tell them what and how to believe. And Paul is submitting his resume. The Lord is Paul's only judge (4:4).

26. To conjure Audre Lorde's (*Sister Outsider*) words.

God is a God who shames the wise and strong of the world with what it considers foolish and weak, but humans should not boast (3:21). Again, Paul has no interest in the human Jesus, only in the Christ of faith.[27] The Corinthian believers should resonate with Paul's argument, since few of them are wise, powerful, or of noble birth, according to the flesh (1:26); divide and conquer. Paul is looking for a majority or dominant consensus to support his argument of the binary between human and divine wisdom, knowledge, and speech. The majority of the Corinthian believers are among the insignificant, foolish, and despised that God chose (1:28). Paul sees the Corinthian believers as his beloved children who can have many guardians (παιδαγωγούς) but only one father (πατέρας) (4:14–16). Apollos can be a guardian (a task or position often fulfilled by enslaved persons or socially inferior persons), but he cannot be the patriarch of the Corinthian believers; he is not their daddy, nor their surrogate mother.

When he was a child, James Baldwin's best school friend, who considered himself saved, took Baldwin to his church on a Saturday morning and introduced him to his pastor. Baldwin wrote this of the encounter:

> My friend took me into the back room to meet his pastor—a woman. There she sat, in her robes, smiling, an extremely proud and handsome woman, with Africa, Europe, and the American of the American Indian blended in her face. She was perhaps forty-five or fifty at this time, and in our world she was a very celebrated woman. My friend was about to introduce me when she looked at me and smiled and said, "Whose little boy are you?" Now this, unbelievably, was precisely the phrase used by pimps and racketeers on the Avenue when they suggested, both humorously and intensely, that I "hang out" with them. Perhaps part of the terror they had caused me to feel came from the fact that I unquestionably want to be *somebody's* little boy. . . . It was my good luck—perhaps—that I found myself in the church racket instead of some other and surrendered to a spiritual

27. I appreciate Allen Callahan making this point poignantly as guest lecturer in my New Testament Interpretation course in the Spring of 2022.

seduction long before I came to any carnal knowledge. For when the pastor asked me, with that marvellous [*sic*] smile, "Whose little boy are you?" my heart replied at once, "Why, yours."[28]

In relationships of perceived or actual ownership of subordinates, including within patriarchal (and matriarchal) family and/or fictive kinship hierarchical structures (including civic and social associations and religious institutions), the dominant member, the head or master, controls the construction, production, and dissemination of knowledge to subordinates (i.e., wife, children, students, enslaved persons).

As a young boy, Frederick Douglass's slave mistress, Mrs. Auld, taught him the alphabet and how to spell, until master Auld discovered it. Auld scolded his wife, asserting that a slave need only know how to obey his master and to do what he is told.[29] Douglass "now understood what had been to me a most perplexing difficulty—to wit, the white man's power [knowledge] to enslave the black man, . . . [and] the pathway from slavery to freedom."[30] What Auld "most dreaded," Douglass "most desired" and would achieve at any cost; what Auld considered a "great evil," Douglass considered a "great good."[31] Auld's vehement opposition to his wife teaching Douglass to read—book knowledge—made Douglass determined to learn, and he did so, strategically.[32] The Bible was not the first book Douglass learned to read. He obtained a book entitled *The Columbia Orator* that contained dialogues and speeches supporting emancipation of the enslaved, which he read insatiably until the discontentment

---

28. Baldwin, *The Fire Next Time*, 28–29.

29. Douglass, *Slave Narratives*, 303.

30. Douglass, *Slave Narratives*, 304.

31. Douglass, *Slave Narratives*, 304.

32. Douglass (*Slave Narrative*, 307) befriended "all the little white boys" he met in the street and "converted" them into being his teachers; when running errands for his master that required going any distance, Douglass would carry his book with him and complete one leg of the journey more quickly than usual so he would have time for a reading lesson on his return trip without arousing suspicion; or he would trade bread for a reading lessons from poor starving neighborhood children.

that Master Hugh Auld predicted and feared permeated his soul.[33] Douglass wrote, "I would at times feel that learning to read had been a curse rather than a blessing. It had given me a view of my wretched condition without the remedy."[34] His eyes were opened to the awful crater but provided no ladder for escape. The agony caused him to envy the stupidity of fellow enslaved persons. Douglass desperately wanted to stop thinking. But he could not put the proverbial genie back in the bottle.[35] Reading or knowledge brought into greater relief the condition of Douglass's enslavement; freedom appeared and disappeared, haunting all his senses. His knowledge of freedom came from books, books some would consider secular. When Douglas wanted to know what the word *abolition* meant, he found it in the dictionary where it was defined as "the act of abolishing." But abolish what? From city papers, conversations he listened in on, and other stolen opportunities, Douglass pieced together the meaning.[36] Over the years, Douglas strategically learned to write. He considered it "the will of God" that the enslaved should learn to read; it was both an intellectual and moral endeavor.[37] It was God's will that the enslaved obtain book knowledge. Douglas did not possess a bifurcated concept of knowledge as spiritual/sacred or worldly/secular.

In the Sabbath School Douglass started in the home of a free colored man, forty enslaved men and women attended. Douglass referred to them as "scholars," "ardently desiring to learn," whose "minds had been starved by their cruel masters, . . . shut up in mental darkness."[38] As Douglass taught his fellow enslaved women and men to read using the Bible, he questioned God's absence and lack of action.[39] Education and enslavement, Douglass wisely wrote, are incompatible.[40]

---

33. Douglass, *Slave Narrative*, 307–8.

34. Douglass, *Save Narrative*, 308.

35. Douglass, *Slave Narrative*, 308.

36. Douglass, *Slave Narrative*, 309–10.

37. Douglass, *Slave Narrative*, 337.

38. Douglass, *Slave Narrative*, 337.

39. Douglass, *Slave Narrative*, 337.

40. Douglass, *Slave Narrative*, 305.

Paul argues that God's wisdom is not the wisdom of the world. In fact, the world does not know (οὐκ ἔγνω ὁ κοσμός) God's wisdom (1:21–23). The two are incompatible; one cancels out the other; they do not coexist peacefully. The epistemologies of Black women and men do not reflect this Pauline teaching, even when they quote Paul. Maria Stewart quoted the apostle Paul often, as Lisa Bowens notes in *African American Readings of Paul*.[41] However, Stewart did not follow Paul down his every epistemic rabbit hole. She did not treat formal education or scholarly endeavors as distinct from or at odds with a "religious spirit," as the following quote from her 1833 farewell speech (where she also quotes 1 Cor 3:6) to Boston friends shows:

> In the 15th century, the general spirit of this period is worthy of observation. We might then have seen women preaching and mixing themselves in controversies. Women occupying the chairs of Philosophy and Justice; women haranguing in Latin before the Pope; women writing in Greek and studying in Hebrew; nuns were poetesses and women of quality divines; and young girls who had studied eloquence would, with the sweetest countenances and the most plaintiff voices, pathetically exhort the Pope and the Christian princes to declare war against the Turks. Women in those days devoted their leisure hours to contemplation and study. The religious spirit which has animated women in all ages, showed itself at this time. It has made them by turns, martyrs, apostles, warriors, and concluded in making divines and scholars. Why cannot a religious spirit animate us now? Why cannot we become divines and scholars?[42]

So often churches require or expect learned, skilled, educated professionals to leave their expertise and knowledge—their intellect and unorthodox curiosity—inside the baptismal pool, surrendering all reasoning to the pastor or to denominational creeds. But historically Black women and men understand unmitigated freedom, including in terms of knowledge acquisition and intellectual curiosity, as Godly or Divine. In 1894 George Washington Carver became the

---

41. Bowens, *African American Readings of Paul*.

42. Stewart, "Mrs. Stewart's Farewell Address."

first African American to earn a bachelor's degree in science. In 1874, at the age of ten or eleven, George left the farm of his enslavers, Moses and Susan Carver—where he had been born into slavery in 1864 during the Civil War—to attend a Black school in nearby Neosho, Missouri. In Neosho, a poor African American couple, Mariah and Andrew Watkins, befriended and sheltered George in their home in exchange for household chores. The Watkins had no children of their own; she was a midwife and washed clothes for a living. Mr. Watkins did odd jobs. While in their home, George received formal schooling for the first time in his life. In 1876, George Carver left the Watkins's home in pursuit of more knowledge. He had questions like "Would a flower change its color if its seed were changed?" George didn't leave the Watkins's home empty-handed. Aunt Mariah gave George a beautiful Bible and charged him to use whatever knowledge he gained for the benefit of his people. The one-hundred-plus-year-old Bible that Aunt Mariah gifted Carver was one of the most expensive money could buy; it contained a dictionary, concordance, references, and other study helps. By sending Carver off with their blessings and a Bible, in search of knowledge, Aunt Mariah seeded in George the wholistic view of religion, wisdom, and formal education and of God, science, and a commitment to human flourishing. We do ourselves, our communities, the world, and God a disservice when we construct theologies that pit God against science and formal education. In his earliest letters, Dr. Carver wrote that he "relied on intuition and divine revelation for his scientific insights. Rational thought was for him a way of confirming and illustrating truths that had been attained mystically."[43] Carver once asserted, "I never have to grope for methods: the method is revealed at the moment I am inspired to create something new."[44] God inspires creativity and innovation, but we must give God something to work with. Carver believed that the more information one acquires, the greater the inspiration.[45]

---

43. Kremer, *George Washington Carver*, 145.

44. Kremer, *George Washington Carver*, 146.

45. Kremer, *George Washington Carver*, 146–47.

Paul concludes his discourse on human versus divine speech, knowledge, and wisdom, with the mention of himself and Apollos by name as ministers through whom the Corinthians believed. But the grace of God given to Paul constitutes the gospel foundation on which others (including Apollos) have built (3:4–10). When Paul describes the life of an apostle, readers should also imagine Apollos as an apostle; he too was the object of the world's (and Paul's) gaze (4:9). They are poor, hungry, thirsty, poorly clothed, beaten, and homeless, but they never retaliate (4:6–9). They are like the filth and feces of the world, the foolish (4:13).

SUPERIORITY OF SPIRITUAL KNOWLEDGE: APOLLOS'S STORY IN ACTS AMONG PRO-SLAVERY ADVOCATES

Apollos is a threat to Paul in 1 Corinthians, but anti-slavery advocates deployed Apollos's story in the Acts of the Apostles to demonstrate the absence of humility among pro-slavery advocates. Conversely, pro-slavery advocates weaponized Apollos's story in Acts to support the superiority of white spiritual knowledge and the evangelization of the enslaved. The most foolish and impoverished white Christian man could teach Black enslaved persons. U.S. pro-slavery advocates found the Apollos story in Acts useful for encouraging poor uneducated whites to participate in the evangelization of enslaved Black peoples. In his sermons, Thomas Bacon (1711–68), a white Anglican priest and pro-slavery advocate, proclaimed that it was the duty of white enslavers/masters to save the souls of enslaved Black people through evangelization. Their souls could be saved while their bodies remained enslaved.[46] Bacon knows of many biblical examples, but he selected the story of Apollos in Acts 18:24–26 to make his point:

> Pious, unlearned persons, who, without the help of miracles, or any extraordinary gifts, have, by God's blessing upon their devout endeavors, done much good in this way. Apollos was a man eloquent and mighty in the

46. See Smith, "U.S. Colonial Missions to African Slaves."

scriptures; and being fervent in spirit, spake [*sic*] boldly in the synagogue of the Jews, and taught diligently the things of the Lord, but only knew the baptism of John:— whom when Aquila and Priscilla (a man and his wife who were both Lay-People had heard, they took him unto them, and expounded unto him the way of God more perfectly:—thus becoming, through the grace of the Almighty, blessed instruments of confirming and perfecting the faith of this great man, who thenceforth became of the chief and boldest champions in the cause of Christianity.—Let this example, my brethren, encourage you to do the likewise:—throw aside all fears of disappointment: —teach your poor benighted slaves as much as you know yourselves:—and freely hold forth that light of the gospel which you so freely have received:—rest the success upon the grace and goodness of Almighty God, praying for his blessing upon your pious endeavors:—and where you find yourselves at any loss, consult your minister, or such good Books as you may have an opportunity of procuring, and doubt not of receiving extraordinary helps from that blessed spirit which our Savior hath promised shall remain in his Church forever.[47]

Indeed, Aquila and Priscilla/Prisca are equated with poor unlearned white men, but enslavers never imagined Black bodies as eloquent or wise and prohibited them from becoming literate. William Fitzgerald argues that we find continuity between depictions and ideologies about the enslaved [and enslavers] in ancient and modern literature. He writes that "the literary servant does not seem to change with the times."[48] The ideo-theological separation of soul from body soothed the consciences of white Christians and/ or enslavers. White enslavers could continue to reap the material, social, and economic benefits of enslaving Black people—by any means necessary—while convincing themselves that if they saved Black people's souls, they would avoid God's judgment.[49]

47. Bacon and Meade, *Sermons Addressed to Masters and Servants*, 56–57.

48. Fitzgerald, "The Slave, between Absence and Presence," 249. See Robbins, *The Servant's Hand*.

49. Bacon and Meade, *Sermons Addressed to Masters and Servant*, 41. In

Christian slave masters would reap great benefits from teaching the enslaved "the doctrines of Christ." Initially, many enslavers refused to convert the enslaved, fearing the enslaved would become unmanageable and discontent, as noted above with Douglass. The enslaved would expect freedom and want the same rights and privileges granted to white people. Bacon rebuffs their excuses and objections. In objection number six, Bacon asserts that some white enslavers object on the grounds that they themselves are too ignorant and lacking in knowledge.[50] Notably, when uneducated white enslavers resist evangelization of the enslaved on the basis of their own ignorance, Bacon deploys the story of the encounter between Apollos, Prisca, and Aquila in Acts to demonstrate that if the ignorant, unlearned, and materially poor (i.e., Prisca and Aquilla) are called to teach even the educated and eloquent (i.e., Apollos), certainly uneducated and uninformed white people can teach illiterate enslaved Black people. Black people are the low hanging fruit. Bacon, like Paul in 1 Corinthians, distinguishes between spiritual (or Divine) knowledge and formal education (worldly knowledge) and argues that white enslavers only need sufficient (spiritual) knowledge to ensure that through God's grace their own souls go to heaven and that they practice what little they know. Bacon uses the Apollos narrative to distinguish between spiritual knowledge and knowledge gained through formal education and to prioritize the former over the latter. Thus, constructed whitened spiritual knowledge always trumps formal education and Black knowledge production. Even "ignorant" white Christian men could claim epistemic superiority over all Black peoples. This constructed socialized ideology remains with us, as demonstrated by white Christian nationalism. In this

Bacon's third sermon on Colossians 4:1, he revisits two points from his first sermon on that verse: (1) "all Christian masters and mistresses" are obligated "to bring up their slaves in the knowledge and fear of God"; (2) enslavers (masters and mistresses) will reap material and spiritual advantages or blessings from fulfilling this duty, including the "arrest of God's judgment" and hiding "a multitude of sins."

50. Bacon and Meade, *Sermons Addressed to Masters and Servants*, 54–57.

twenty-first century, young white high school dropouts are as likely to find employment as college-educated Black women and men.[51]

Bacon, and other white Christian ministers, missionaries, and/or enslavers eventually viewed enslaved Blackened heathenized bodies as the ideal objects of white evangelization.[52] When white Christians taught the gospel to enslaved Black bodies, the latter were both "ingrafted into [white] families . . . [and became] part *of the household of faith*" while their place as enslaved peoples in the master's household remained unchanged.[53] The household of faith was not distinct from enslavers'/masters' households. The enslaved had souls that could only be saved through the constructed spiritual knowledge that white enslavers possessed by virtue of sanctified whiteness and their access to literacy and formal education. And this whitened mediated spiritual knowledge trumped and superseded any knowledge that the enslaved and/or unsaved achieved through informal or formal education.

The placing of a greater valuation on constructed spiritual knowledge above worldly knowledge attracted some enslaved (and freed) Black people who were denied access to book learning, writing skills, and/or formal education, and understandably so. It can be empowering and humanizing to accept Paul's binary epistemic logic when one is already considered subordinate and/or inferior in an existing hierarchy or in a racialized society where the subordinated are denied or limited in their access to literacy, formal education, and/or book knowledge. The idea that one can claim access to knowledge through God or God's Spirit that is superior to the world's knowledge and wisdom can be appealing when a society's educational systems are not established for, not physically located or accessible to, and/or not structured in terms of policy, pedagogy or curriculum with Black and other nonwhite or poor people in mind or are built to intentionally exclude, deter, or sabotage their entrance, progress, or success.

51. Adams, "White High School Drop-Outs."

52. Bacon and Meade, *Sermons Addressed to Masters and Servants*, 49.

53. Bacon and Meade, *Sermons Addressed to Masters and Servants*, 54.

In the mind of Bacon and other white Christian preachers and enslavers, enslaved Black people should only be regarded as unthinking receivers and imitators of white or whitened (even impoverished, insufficient, and incompetent) knowledge, but never as producers of knowledge. Bacon advises white masters and mistresses that if they conduct their lives according to the knowledge they already have, they "can surely communicate it to others [i.e., the enslaved], as easily as you could shew them how to handle a hoe, a spade, or other implement of husbandry (farming), whose use you are acquainted with, or teach them any sort of manufacture you are able to perform yourselves."[54]

Further Bacon argues that even unlearned, ignorant, and poor white men have enough knowledge to "bring your own souls to heaven, through the grace of God" by living into what they already know.[55] But if they think their knowledge is deficient, they can always "seek after" and attain spiritual knowledge; it is more important than any material gain the world offers.[56] This constructed binary also maintains and guarantees the superiority and dominance of elite educated white men or poor white people. The worst excuse white masters and mistresses offered for neglecting the souls of the enslaved was ignorance, especially since they reside in a "*Christian* country, where you have [white] ministers to instruct you."[57] If white enslavers desire to know more, they have no excuse, since they have access to plenty of white Christians to educate them. Bacon argued that religious ignorance is the worst kind of ignorance.[58] Thus, spiritual knowledge is superior to other forms of knowledge. Yet, elite white people had access to and controlled *both* spiritual *and* secular knowledge and took full advantage of the latter. Persons and/or communities who assert that the spiritual is subordinate to the material world while also claiming the authority and power to define and evaluate what constitutes the spiritual or

---

54. Bacon and Meade, *Sermons Addressed to Masters and Servants*, 55.

55. Bacon and Meade, *Sermons Addressed to Masters and Servants*, 55.

56. Bacon and Meade, *Sermons Addressed to Masters and Servants*, 55.

57. Bacon and Meade, *Sermons Addressed to Masters and Servants*, 55.

58. Bacon and Meade, *Sermons Addressed to Masters and Servants*, 56.

Godly create a hierarchical power structure that always places them at the top and all others and their epistemologies squarely in the fleeting inferior material world.

In response to Bacon and other pro-slavery advocates, the abolitionist William Lloyd Garrison deployed the story of Apollos to demonstrate the humility that pro-slavery advocates should have demonstrated.[59] Garrison was not wrong about Apollos. In Acts, Apollos demonstrates not just humility, but deference toward Prisca and Aquila. Apollos may not have been commissioned by either the Jerusalem or Antioch (Syrian) assemblies of Christ-believers. Thus, Apollos may have been treated as subordinate to Paul in the similar way that Paul is subordinated to the Jerusalem Council and church (assembly) in Acts (see Acts chapters 13 and 15).

The Witness of Acts about Apollos and Paul

Although the Acts of the Apostles was written about half a century or more after (early second century CE) Paul wrote 1 Corinthians, information we find in Acts about Apollos supports his depiction and popularity in Paul's letter and perhaps supplies additional reliable information collected from Luke's sources. In Acts, Apollos is identified as an Alexandrian Jewish man who is a member of the Jesus movement. He is described as a man of eloquent speech (ἀνὴρ λόγιος) who arrived in Ephesus already capable of powerfully expounding the Scriptures (18:24). Further, Apollos had been instructed (by whom, we do not know) in the way of the Master/ Lord (τὴν ὁδὸν τοῦ κυρίου).[60] If Apollos was among the Egyptians present at Pentecost, he was not baptized after Peter's Pentecost speech, for he had only received the baptism of John when he encountered Prisca and Aquilla (2:10; 18:25b). We do not know who taught Apollos about Jesus, but whoever taught him did not require that he receive the baptism of Jesus.[61] Apollos is also described as

59. Johnson, *William Lloyd Garrison and His Times*.

60. Conversely, in Galatians Paul claims that no human being instructed him (Gal 1:1—2:10).

61. Presumably, Ananias's baptism of Saul/Paul in Acts was the baptism of

zealous in the spirit; he taught accurately the things concerning Jesus, despite knowing only the baptism of John (18:25; cf. Rom 12:11). According to tradition, Jesus baptized no one. Perhaps, unlike Paul, Apollos knew the historical Jesus. One does not have to be baptized in Jesus's name first to receive the Spirit's anointing in Acts (10:44–48).

In Ephesus, Apollos begins speaking boldly in the synagogues (18:26). The Greek verb παρρησιάζομαι, which is translated boldly or courageously, is the same verb (or the noun form παρρησία) that describes bold apostolic preaching in Acts, particularly in precarious situations. It characterizes the proclamation of the Twelve, particularly Peter and John, as well as Paul, Barnabas, and Apollos (9:27–28; 13:8–13, 46; 14:3). I argue that this characterization of Apollos's preaching signifies that he too was an apostle, and 1 Corinthians implicitly agrees. Apollos was a disciple of John, and also an apostle.

Does Apollos, as an eloquent Alexandrian Jewish man, find himself in a precarious situation in Ephesus, in the diaspora, and in Prisca and Aquila's presence? Ronald Charles asserts that "a diasporic space must always be problematized in terms of race, racism, religion, class, gender, sexuality, education, and so on."[62] In Ephesus, Paul's coworkers in the manual labor of tentmaking (8:1–4) pull Apollos aside to explain to him *more* accurately the way of God (18:26; cf. 16:17; 19:9, 23; 24:22), despite the prior knowledge and skill he brings to the preaching of the gospel.[63] Interestingly, in Acts, Prisca and Aquilla are never depicted as participating in the preaching of the gospel in the synagogues with Paul; they are only co-laborers, it appears, in the tentmaking trade (Acts 18:1–4;

Jesus, but it is not specifically named as such; shortly after the baptism Saul is preaching Jesus (9:16, 20; cf. 2:38).

62. Charles, *Paul and the Politics of Diaspora.*

63. Is an epistemological distinction being made between "the way of the Lord" and "the way of God"? See Smith, *The Literary Construction of the Other in the Acts of the Apostles.* Both phrases are unique to this story in Acts. Throughout Acts, the phrase is simply "the Way" (19:9, 23; 24:22). The only other deviation of the term "the Way" is spoken by the Pythian slave girl who says that Paul and Silas proclaim the way of salvation (16:17).

cf. Rom 16:3). The couple's encounter with Apollos provides an epistemological opportunity to disseminate spiritual knowledge, an opportunity that had so far escaped them.

Why does Apollos show deference to Prisca and Aquila, without hesitation, given his reputation for teaching the Scriptures accurately, knowledge of the "way of the Lord," and eloquence? Was Apollos identified as the social inferior of Prisca and Aquila and thus obligated to show deference toward them? Is it possible that Apollos is a formerly enslaved man, a diaspora Jewish freedman, as well as an apostle?[64] Robin Thompson convincingly argues that the synagogue of the libertines/freedmen that opposed Stephen in Acts 6:8–15 likely consisted of diaspora Jewish freedmen from Alexandria, Cyrene, Cilicia, and Asia who because of their separation from the temple before living in Judea "might be more zealous concerning the law of Moses and the institution of the temple than even the native Jewish population."[65] Was Apollos a member of the Synagogue of the Libertines/Freedman? Could he also have been among the Jewish slaves and freedmen ousted from Rome in 54 CE about the same time that Prisca and Aquila and all Jews were expelled (Acts 18:1–4)? Is it possible that Apollos shows deference toward Prisca and Aquila because he is recognized (or somehow known) to be a stigmatized freedman and the couple are freeborn Jews? If Apollos is a freedman, he would have found common ground with the freed population of Roman Corinth, giving him a possible advantage among the Corinthians and putting Paul at a disadvantage.

64. Martin (*Apollos: Paul's Partner or Rival?*) argues that Paul defected from Alexandria demonstrating disloyalty to his family and ethnic group. Wilson ("Apostle Apollos?," 334) concludes that the apostle Paul regarded Apollos as an apostle: "We can . . . conclude, with a high degree of probability, that Paul regarded Apollos, the Alexandrian Jew who was competent in the Scriptures and subsequently went to preach and teach in Corinth, as a fellow apostle who, along with Paul and others, became a fool for the Messiah."

65. Thompson, "Diaspora Jewish Freedmen: Stephen's Deadly Opponents," 175, 176. Is it possible that the "way of the Lord" implies a zeal for "the law of Moses" that requires gentile circumcision where the "way of God" taught by Prisca and Aquila proclaims God's grace for the gentiles (see Acts 18:25, 27; cf. 15:19)?

Why did Apollos need letters to cross into Achaia or Corinth (18:27–28)? First-century Corinth, as a Roman province, was a city populated with formerly enslaved persons (see chapter 2), and it was where Aquila and Prisca landed after being forced from Rome (18:1–4). Perhaps, that is why Apollos desired to visit Corinth and attracted a significant following there; he was a knowledgeable, gifted orator, and, perhaps, a freedman among other freedpersons. He would have been a source of pride and boasting among other freedpersons and even the enslaved. It is also possible as George Barton argues, that "the Corinthians regarded Apollos's teaching as much more intellectual [and powerful] than St. Paul's."[66]

Why would an eloquent Jewish man from Alexandria humble himself to be taught by a Jewish couple not as erudite as himself, unless he were of a lower class? Could Apollos have been sent from Alexandria by his patron, a member of the Jesus movement, to preach in the diaspora, given his exceptional skills? Even a skilled freedman could be considered and treated as a social inferior to a poor freeborn man. Den Dulk convincingly argues that Apollos's submission to Aquila and Prisca is significant given negativity attached to Aquila's Pontic identity. He argues that Pontics were stereotypically understood to be ignorant or unlearned peoples, lacking sophistication, and savage barbarians.[67] The scene of Prisca and Aquilla teaching Apollos, according to Den Dulk, demonstrates a reversal, as in Luke's Gospel, when the sophisticated Apollos from Alexandria, Egypt is taught by the Pontic Aquila who with his wife is also a manual laborer; it "may be regarded as Luke's way of putting Apollos [Paul's rival] in his place,"[68] so as not to steal Paul's thunder. I have argued elsewhere, Apollos's eloquence elevates him in the eyes of aristocratic Romans. As a Roman citizen, according

66. Barton, "Some Influences of Apollos in the New Testament," 208. Contrary to Barton, we cannot unequivocally conclude that Apollos never founded/planted an assembly of believers (Acts 18:24–28).

67. Den Dulk, "Aquila and Apollos."

68. Den Dulk ("Aquila and Apollos," 186, 187 [quote]) argues that Luke's primary "goal in juxtaposing the man from Pontus and the man from Alexandria had more to do with subverting negative stereotypes about people from Pontus."

to Acts, Paul would also know the value of eloquence among the Roman elites.[69]

In Corinth, Apollos powerfully influenced the existing believers, but he also convinced nonbelievers that Jesus is the Messiah. Apollos planted *and* watered (cf. 18:27–28). When Paul arrives in Ephesus, he discovers disciples already there (likely disciples who responded to Apollos's preaching) whom he baptizes because they had only received the baptism of John. Why is it that Prisca and Aquila do not baptize Apollos in the name of Jesus, given that he only knows the baptism of John? The subordination of Apollos seems most significant. In Ephesus Paul watered some seeds that Apollos planted. According to Titus 3:13, Apollos significantly impacted the Jesus movement in Corinth and beyond.[70] But Paul is not one for biodiversity among apostles unless a hierarchy is established that places him as the sole or chief patriarch and planter.

In 1 Corinthians 1:18—2:16, Paul places eloquent wisdom and baptismal success in opposition to the gospel to diminish Apollos's reputation and to disband the assemblies bearing his name to create a unified body of believers under his apostleship.[71] When Paul identifies himself as the planter and Apollos as the one who waters at 3:6, he subordinates water baptism to preaching the gospel (often equated with planting seeds in the gospels). Paul's metaphor also reinforces order; seeds are planted first. Even if Paul preached in Corinth first, an apostle arriving after Paul could have preached to different audiences who became believers, and vice versa.[72] For Paul

69. Smith, *Womanist Sass and Talk Back*, esp. ch. 4, "Epistemologies, Pedagogies, and the Subordinated Other."

70. Barton ("Some Influences of Apollos in the New Testament," 208–9) attempts to trace Apollos's influence through Philonic thought processes and ideas, including Philo's philosophy of logos, narrative of births of extraordinary people, his eschatology, and his allegorical interpretations of the OT. Archer ("Apollos and the Logos Doctrine," 301–3) also attributes a logos doctrine to Apollos; Spicq, "L'Épitre aux Hébreux."

71. See Miller, "Not with Eloquent Wisdom."

72. Some scholars have attempted to reconstruct Apollos's philosophy through an examination of Alexandrian antecedents, including the logos doctrine in Philo of Alexandria, or by arguing that Apollos is the author the NT book of Hebrews. See Barton, "Some Influences of Apollos"; Archer, "Apollos

(or Luke), Witherington argues "baptism is not a means of conversion, nor is it necessary for conversion."[73] But planting the seeds of the gospel is necessary. Nothing happens unless seeds are planted. Paul's description of Apollos as one who waters is Paul's rhetorical attempt to construct an image of Apollos as subordinate within a hierarchy of evangelization or knowledge production and dissemination. Paul implicitly undermines Apollos, rather than directly attack him.[74] This is Paul's *modus operandi* throughout 1 Corinthians. Whether he was aware of it or not, Apollos planted/preached the gospel in contested spaces.

Enslaved and freed Black mothers, grandmothers, great-grandmothers, and other mothers often gardened in contested spaces. Our mothers, grandmothers, and other mothers planted, watered, cultivated, and curated their gardens in the multi-functional contested spaces around the cabins of the enslaved and in tiny and large spaces in freedom. Alice Walker described her mother's garden this way:

> My mother adorned with flowers whatever shabby house we were forced to live in. And not just your typical straggly country stand of zinnias, either. She planted ambitious gardens—and still does—with over fifty different varieties of plants that bloom profusely from early March until late November. Before she left home for the fields, she watered her flowers, chopped up the grass and laid out new beds. . . . Whatever she planted grew as if by magic and her fame as a grower of flowers spread over three counties. Because of her creativity with her flowers, even my memories of poverty are seen through a screen of blooms—sunflowers, petunias, roses, dahlias, forsythia, spirea. . . . And so on, . . . whatever rocky soil she landed on, she turned into a garden. A garden so brilliant with colors, so original in its design, so magnificent with life and creativity, that to this day people drive by our house in Georgia—perfect

---

and the Logos Doctrine"; Lo Bue, "The Historical Background of the Epistle to the Hebrews"; Montefiore, *The Epistle to the Hebrews.*

73. Witherington, *Conflict and Community in Corinth,* 104.

74. Ker, "Paul and Apollos," 96.

strangers and imperfect strangers—and ask to stand or
walk among my mother's art.[75]

Those who heard and responded to Apollos's preaching wit-
nessed in him the art of eloquent preaching. Paul's last mention of
Apollos in 1 Corinthians 16:12 states as follows: "Now concerning
our brother Apollos, I strongly urged him to visit you with the other
brothers, but it was not God's will for him to come now. He will
come when he has the opportunity" (cf. Titus 3:13). Mihaila asserts
that Apollos and Paul labored independently and not necessar-
ily in competition, given the familial language used.[76] Conversely,
Margaret Mitchell asserts we cannot determine from the language
of 16:12 that Paul and Apollos were on "good terms, but only that
Paul wishes to give that impression."[77] Fictive kinship language seldom mitigated the social class divisions or abuses leveled against
perceived or constructed social inferiors, especially those that
inhabited stigmatized bodies (e.g., the enslaved and freedwomen
and freedmen).[78] As Benny Tat-Siong Liew argues Paul "is building community [unity] on the backs of those whom 'everyone' [so
he hopes] can agree to marginalize and stigmatize."[79] Enslaved and
even freedpersons would find Paul's teachings difficult, and even
stifling of any social mobility they might desire to achieve by ac-
quiring so-called worldly skills, wisdom, or knowledge.

The construction of human knowledge as sacred or secular
by a person of authority or a dominant group or institution with
control of resources to set the boundaries of knowledge, determine
how it is accessed, make themselves the source or resource of that
knowledge, and decide what it looks like to master and imitate that
knowledge has a marginalizing and exclusionary impact on persons or groups that rely on the dominant for access, assessment,

75. Walker, *In Our Mothers' Gardens*, 241.

76. Mihaila, *The Paul-Apollos Relationship and Paul's Stance toward Greco-
Roman Rhetoric*, 212.

77. Mitchell, *Paul and the Rhetoric of Reconciliation*, 293.

78. See Smith, "Utility, Fraternity, and Reconciliation," 47–48.

79. Liew, "Redressing Bodies in Corinth," 75–97. See also Smith, "Hagar
Still *Ain't* Free"; Parker, "Feminized-Minoritized Paul?"

and validation. The situation is merciless and annihilating when the dominant function within structures and systems that constitute a web of intersectional oppressions including racism, sexism, queerphobia, classism. Katie Cannon found herself in such a web as a doctoral student in Bible when the Hebrew Bible department at Union Theological Seminary (New York) dropped her from the program; the white male professors determined that Cannon was not a "serious enough student" because she ministered as a supply pastor while in the doctoral program.[80] Cannon's participation in the church was considered irreconcilable with the pursuit of an academic degree in Hebrew Bible.

In 1 Corinthians Paul attempts to construct an epistemological web that diminishes the intellectual capital of Apollos, those who follow him, and other folks like him (e.g., perhaps Chloe and other freedpersons) who may already be or might arise as theo-political party leaders like Apollos in Corinth. That matrix of spiritual knowledge that Paul constructs renders invisible Paul's fears and biases and the "worldly knowledge" on which he now relies, that shaped him and his thinking. The assertion that a divine knowledge exists apart from human knowledge is a human construct. The content of so-called divine knowledge is a human construct, constructed for and by humans who make claims about divine inspiration. Divine inspiration does not bypass the human subject, whether that subject is the apostle Paul, Apollos, Chloe of Corinth, Maria Stewart, or George Washington Carver.

---

80. Weems, "The Biblical Field's Loss Was Womanist Ethics' Gain."

CHAPTER 4

Hands Off Our Hair, Paul!

Reading Quarely and Transgressively to Shatter the Glass Ceiling Placed on Our Heads

"What else, then, is required? Why was it that, when I meditated and sought the escape hatch at the top of my brain, which, at an earlier stage of growth, I had been fortunate enough to find, I now encountered a ceiling, as if the route to merge with the infinite I had become used to was plastered over? One day after I had asked this question earnestly for half a year, it occurred to me that in my physical self there remained one last barrier to my spiritual liberation, at least in the present phase: *my hair*."
ALICE WALKER, "OPPRESSED HAIR PUTS A CEILING ON THE
BRAIN," 285 (MY EMPHASIS)

"Quare (Kwâr) n. meaning queer; also, opp. of straight; odd or slightly off kilter; from the African American vernacular for queer; sometimes homophobic in usage, but always denotes excess incapable of being contained within conventional categories of being.... One for whom sexual and gender identities always already intersect with racial subjectivity.
...Quare is to queer as 'reading' is to 'throwing shade."
E. PATRICK JOHNSON[1]

1. Johnson, "'Quare' Studies," 125.

Black women, men, and their children who elect to wear their hair natural, long or short, gender nonconforming or not, still experience discrimination, primarily in dominant white spaces where they work, play, and/or attend school. When Black women submit or assimilate to constructed gender norms for women's hairstyles, they do so primarily for two reasons: they find their natural hair easier to maintain when it is chemically or otherwise straightened, and/or they desire to mitigate or avoid the racism (i.e., micro- and macro-aggressions from negative comments to physical abuse) that considers Black natural hair unprofessional, undesirable, and/or unkempt. Many Black people have elected to exercise respectability politics. Failure to assimilate to the expectations of the dominant can result in not getting or losing a desired and/or necessary job, harassment on a job or at school, or expulsion from school or a school event. Also, short hair, for all women and particularly for Black women, is still generally considered less feminine and/or male-gendered, especially among people who love patriarchy and among many religious folks.

In the 1960s and 1970s, Black natural hair, especially the afros and locs, was viewed as militant by some Black and nonBlack people, many of whom still insist on this connection. A Black woman, man, or child proudly wearing their natural hair is seen as someone who cannot be controlled (as if we must be controlled) or as nonconformist. Few Black women celebrities wear natural Black hairstyles, most wear long flowing weaves or wigs, publicly, partly because of industry biases against Black natural hair and preferences for long straight tresses. But when high-profile successful Black women routinely and unapologetically wear Black natural hairstyles, Black women feel proudly affirmed. Many Black women burst with pride because the first Black woman U.S. Supreme Court justice, Ketanji Brown Jackson, wears her natural dred locs and when actress Viola Davis tossed the straight wigs and weaves for a short-natural 'fro or full-blown afro wig on the red carpet, in an interview or photo shoot. Viola Davis decided to wear her natural hair in her later years of life. Davis stated that she is "embracing who I am . . . [choosing] to live an authentic life, . . . wearing my natural hair is part of that."[2] These public unveilings affirm Black women in their natural blackness, from head to toe. When Justice Ketanji Brown Jackson cracked or shattered a glass ceiling, she did it as a woman of faith in all her natural glorious locs.

Yet, it remains that Black women (and men and children) are ridiculed by persons and institutions outside and within Black communities when their hair styles do not conform to the expectations of the dominant white culture and/or of assimilated Black peoples. Black women fight against white racism *and* "confront and wade through the racist constructs underlying our deprivation of each other."[3] Very short natural hair styles or teeny-weeny afros (twa's) worn by Black women and Black men's long locks are often viewed as *transgendering* or transgressing the gendered boundaries of what is considered acceptable, professional, and normal for men and women. Women's hair should be long or longish and men's hair should be short or shaven. Women's hair must be distinguishable from men's hair, and this distinction is a heterosexual identity marker, more so than distinctive gendered clothing. The length and style of one's hair is often associated with one's gender and sexuality in our society and among many readers of the Scriptures. In 1 Corinthians 11:1–16, Paul connects gender and sexuality with the length of men and women's hair. Paul conceives of gender in binary terms of freeborn man and woman, both of whom are cisgendered heterosexual (i.e., sexual identity assigned at birth and not transgendered), and they, as man and woman, participate in a Divine hierarchical coupling, which he argues reflects or represents the Yahwist Edenic story of God's creation of human beings (Gen 2:4b–25).

According to Paul, the Corinthian believers' hair is symbolic of a Divine gendered hierarchy that subordinates woman to man. The woman whose hair is covered or worn long acknowledges and demonstrates submission to a Divine and natural gendered hierarchy that subordinates woman to man, and to every man. Men should not cover their heads, but generally maintain short or shaven hair

2. Davis, "Interview on Wearing Her Natural Hair."

3. Lorde, *Sister Outsider*, 164.

when praying and prophesying in the assembly of the believers, but the opposite is true for women.

For many contemporary readers Paul's rhetoric functions as the hair salon-police and ultimate authority on women and men's hairstyles. Such readers, following Paul's admonition in 1 Corinthian 11:1–16, preach or teach that women's hair should be long and men's hair short(er); that power is connected especially with a woman's "uncut" hair (whether long or short).[4] With over eighteen thousand subscribers on her natural hair care channel, Black You-Tuber Mrs. Charity Umar posted a video encouraging Black women to refrain from cutting their hair; it attracted over fifteen thousand views.[5] In that video, Umar reads from 1 Corinthians 11:15 and teaches women that a woman's hair is her glory. She argues that when a woman lets her hair grow long, she allows it to glow, to shine, which means "your God-given hair, your natural hair . . . if that hair is long, *then* it manifests glory" (emphasis Umar's). Umar asserts that "long hair is attractive to men and to other women, . . . long hair is beautiful, . . . it ultimately reveals" God's glory and the Creator takes the credit. But, many Black women, men, and children reject Paul's gendered hair logic and the theo-ideology that supports it.

This chapter provides a womanist reading of 1 Corinthians 11:1–16 through the lens of and in conversation with the historical and recent policing and criminalization of Black people's transgressive hairstyles, transgressing and transgendering Pauline theo-ideology and dominant whitened expectations. Increasingly, more Black men, women, and children choose to transgress gendered and racialized norms that insist that Black women and men assimilate to white beauty standards and/or religion-based ideologies that insist that women wear their hair long and/or straightened and men sport short haircuts that are acceptable and respectable to dominant white culture and nonwhite gatekeepers. But Black women and men (and

---

4. See, e.g., Stoneking, "The Power of a Woman's Uncut Hair." He preaches that families are blessed and spared from tragedy because of woman's uncut hair. Stoneking argues for the translation "uncut hair" because some women's hair does not grow long. For him, the key is never to cut it.

5. Umar, "Your Hair Your Glory."

others) who choose to transgress (i.e., disregard, do otherwise, live as fugitives from social or cultural enslavement in the "land of the free") and transgender dominant gendered, racialized, culturally-biased and/or religion-based norms are too often penalized, physically abused, and/or criminalized. For example, two Black male high school teens, Deandre Arnold (who inspired the CROWN Act discussed below) and his cousin Kaden Bradford, were suspended from Barbers Hill High School in Mont Belvieu, Texas for wearing their hair in long natural locks, against school policy. Deandre, whose father is Trinidadian, considers his locs part of his identity and culture.[6] Similarly, sixteen-year-old Andrew Johnson's locs were cut off during a high school wrestling match in 2019.[7]

More Black women are wearing their natural hair in big fros or long and/or towering braided hairstyles. Many are doing the "big chop" (cutting off their chemically processed hair and returning to their natural hair texture) and sporting twa's. Too many such Black women are often policed, censored, and/or masculinized. The censoring takes the form of negative accusations of *transgendering* (being or behaving in ways considered antithetical to gendered norms) or *transgressing* normalized gendered and racialized identity markers inscribed in bodies, the most visible symbol being Black people's hair and clothing. Of course, Black women and men sometimes deliberately elect to *transgress* or *transgender*, to resist and reject, oppressive racialized and gender norms as political expressions of autonomy, individual agency, cultural pride, and/or collective freedom. A queering of 1 Corinthians 11:1–16—disrupting the Pauline binary, throwing shade on his normalized oppressive gendered hierarchy—challenges Paul's sacralized normativity and subverts negative oppressive accusations of *transgendering* to embrace Black people's transgression as authentic, life-giving, sacred, and holistic. To use Joseph Marchal's language, I am on the *verge* of reading queerly, offering "a challenge to regimes of the normal."[8] In one sense, Marchal describes queer as "less an identity and more

6. Edwards, "Court: School District Dress Code Discriminated."

7. Stubbs, "A Wrestler Was Forced to Cut His Dreadlocks before a Match."

8. Marchal, *Bodies on the Verge*, 9.

a disposition, a mode of examining the processes that cast certain people and practices into categories of normal and abnormal and then interrogating the various effects of such processes. Not that a person or a text possesses a quality marked queer but rather that one can queer an arrangement of power and privilege or interpret queerly by attending to certain dynamics."[9] Queering racialized gendered norms and accusations of transgendering and transgressions from an Africana womanist perspective, I am troubling the biblical (or Pauline) waters, to use Cain Hope Felder's words,[10] as a cisgendered heterosexual Black woman who loves her short natural hair. Put different, I am reading "quarely" as a heterosexual Black woman committed to opposing all oppressions, including those based on constructions of race, sexuality, gender, class, and religion.[11] As such I privilege the historical and contemporary experiences of Black women, men, and children, regardless of class, sexual-identity, and religious identity, who wear their 'fros, twa's, twist-outs, shaven heads, and short or long locs freely and unapologetically, regardless of their gender or sexual identity. They *transgress* dominant sacralized societal and inter- and intra-communal ideologies in the act of *transgendering* or rejecting, disrupting, and crossing oppressive normalized and racialized gendered constructs and boundaries inscribed in Black bodies, and that often commence with attempts to control and stigmatize the hair on their heads.

A CLOSER LOOK AT PAUL'S ARGUMENT

In 1 Corinthians 10:31—11:1, we find the immediate prologue to Paul's rhetorical prescriptive head and hair logic in 1 Corinthians 11:2–16. The Corinthian believers are urged to privilege all things (πάντα) that expand or increase the assembly of God, which may conflict with and trump anything that the Corinthian believers consider lawful and personally and culturally beneficial or life-giving (10:23). They should seek to do that which is advantageous

9. Marchal, *Bodies on the Verge*, 10.

10. Felder, *Troubling Biblical Waters*.

11. Johnson, "'Quare' Studies," 125.

to other persons different from themselves, not privileging their own pleasures or desires (10:24). This admonition applies to eating food sold in the marketplace and meals served by unbelievers (but where is the line in the sand?); they should raise no objections to each such meals based on their own conscience (τὴν συνείδησιν) (10:25–27). The Corinthian believers are to ignore their own conscience; they are to ignore their own internal voice of knowledge in order to please the other, privileging the conscience of the other above their own conscience, which, Paul argues, is tantamount to pleasing God (10:28–30). This theo-ideology is radically self-negating. If someone else finds it problematic to eat sacrificial food, Paul instructs "don't eat it" so as to respect the other person's conscience or convictions. Paul argues that it pleases God to subjugate one's own freedom (ἡ ἐλευθερία), to mute one's own convictions or conscience to please another (10:29–30).

This prologue is summed up at verse 10:31 where Paul urges the believers to do everything (πάντα) to or for God's glory. Paul rhetorically attempts to convince the Corinthian believers to suppress or ignore their own ways of knowing, consciousness, and/or conscience and to privilege the epistemologies of others. There is not only a way that men and women should eat and drink to God's glory (in private and public), but also a way that they should pray and prophesy to God's glory when they assemble as believers. Who determines what is pleasing to God? God's recognized authoritative intermediaries or representatives (i.e., apostles, prophets, ancestors), like Paul (the apostle with a podium and a pen or an amanuensis or scribe), decide what is pleasing to God. One way to determine what is pleasing to God is whether or not someone or something (e.g., a men, women, the assembly or church of God) seeks someone else's advantage or their own or follows another's conscience or their own. The Corinthians must not offend God's assembly of believers in seeking their own advantage, just as Paul himself has not sought his own benefit. Paul asserts that he has tried to please everyone else in all things; he offers no exceptions (10:33a); this is an implicit invitation to imitate Paul. The Corinthian believers are being asked to act contrary to their own conscience or ways of knowing in favor of another's conscience, wisdom, and epistemologies, including Paul's! Thus, the Corinthians are to bear the burden of the others' salvation built upon their own self-denial and abasement of their own internal barometer for knowing or deciphering what is pleasing to God (10:33b).

What is the impact of Paul's prescriptive rhetoric on those believers who are already not regarded as producers of knowledge, as being without conscience, as unwise, and/or oppressed (i.e., children, the poor, the unwell, women, wives, formerly enslaved/ freedpersons, enslaved persons, and/or the colonized)? What is the impact of Paul's teaching on the marginalized and muted among the believers whose own consciences and ways of knowing are subjugated to the privilege, desires, needs, and ideologies of men, husbands, enslavers/slave masters, freeborn persons, the wealthy and noble, and/or patrons? They already bear the burden of others' well-being and desires to the exclusion of their own. Their burden is increased.

At 1 Corinthians 11:1, Paul explicitly demands what he only implied in 10:33: Become my imitators, just as I am an imitator of Christ. Give up your agency, consciousness, awareness, and epistemologies (ways of knowledge and knowledge production) for my own. This Pauline rhetoric is prologue to ideologies and practices of power, control, and subjugation. In applauding the Corinthian believers for re-membering him *in everything* and for holding onto (i.e., practicing, imitating, and teaching) the traditions he passed down to them (11:2), Paul describes the ways the Corinthians have already yielded to him as a model for imitating him. Paul wants them to continue the practice of conducting themselves according to traditions they received from him, to trust, uncritically, his guidance and teaching.

Using absolute language (i.e., all or every) Paul reveals his own epistemological desire for the believers: "I wish you to know (θέλω ὑμᾶς εἰδειναι) that Christ is the head (κεφαλή) of every man (παντός ἀνδρός)" (11:3).[12] Further, the man is head of woman,

---

12. Barrett (*Commentary on the First Epistle to the Corinthians*, 249) understands the assertion that Christ is the head of every man as a possible reference to "Christ as the agent of creation"; in the case of man as the head of woman, it means man is the origin of the woman's being (238). See also

and God is head of Christ.[13] Woman is head of no one.[14] The word translated *head* is body language that Paul uses again in chapter 12 of 1 Corinthians to discuss the assembly of believers as a metaphorical body. Contemporary (and perhaps ancient) readers of chapter 11 will associate the head in chapter 12 with the man after having read the former. Paul's speech about all members being of equal importance does not mitigate the hierarchical gendered headship language of chapter 11. Rhetoric about equality does not change one's place in society or the hierarchical relationships that society insists upon and polices.[15]

The communal spaces where the assemblies of God in Corinth gather for worship are, of course to Paul's disappointment, contested space with fractures caused by the formation of diverse groups under leadership other than Paul's, including freedwomen like Chloe (see chapters 2 and 3). Still some Corinthian believers prefer to follow Paul's teachings in their homes/assemblies. The private and the public overlap, mutually reinforce each another, and are equally political, i.e., patriarchal, hierarchical, and concerned with control, management, and distribution of both human and nonhuman members and resources.

Murphy-O'Connor ("Sex and Logic in 1 Corinthians 11:2–16"), who similarly argues that "the man is the 'head' of the woman because he is the source of her being; Paul is thinking in terms of the first creation" (493). But, of course, the Priestly version of creation tells a different story (esp. Gen 1:27–31).

13. Kim (*Christ's Body in Corinth*, 61) argues that Paul's response in 11:4–7 "quotes the hegemonic, patriarchal voice of the opponents . . . to counter it," which Kim believes is a plausible conclusion based on 11:11–12. Kim further asserts that "Paul deconstructs his opponents' gender hierarchy (7:9) through God's power. . . . God's initiative nullifies all human construction of power based on gender hierarchy."

14. Fitzmyer, "Kephale in 1 Corinthians 11:3." Based on his *Thesaurus Linguae Graeca* (*TLG*) search of κεφαλή, Joseph Fitzmyer argued that it can and did mean "one having authority over" in Paul's day.

15. Martin, *The Corinthian Body*. Dale Martin has argued that since Paul regards gender hierarchy as natural, preserving it is necessary for a healthy communal body.

SHAMING THOSE WHO TRANSGRESS THE RESTRICTIONS PLACED UPON THEIR HEADS

Shaming is one mechanism for controlling members of the assembly who transgress or might potentially transgress the rules and/or teachings of the community. Paul asserts that every man (πᾶς ἀνὴρ) who prays or prophesies with his head covered disgraces (καταισχύνει) his head (11:4). The primary problem is the man who covers his head (and conversely, the woman who does not) when praying or prophesying. Richard Oster argues that among the Romans during the early empire and before, material culture plainly evinces "the practice of men covering their heads in the context of prayer and prophecy" as a common display of Roman religiosity.[16] Oster asserts that "since Corinth was itself a Roman colony, there should be little doubt that this aspect of Roman religious practice deserves greater attention."[17] Were some Corinthian men imitating Roman piety toward other gods by covering their heads when participating in imperial worship? If so, were they following that same practice when they prayed and prophesied in the assemblies of Christ-believers? Is 1 Corinthians 11:2–16 also Paul's reaction to that practice? Consequently, women's wearing of the veil and/or of long hair becomes a visible sign of their fidelity to God (as head of Christ Jesus), to Christ Jesus as the (invisible or absentee) head of the assembly of believers, to Paul as Christ's male proxy among the believers, and finally to man as the head of the woman (1 Cor 11:3; 15:12–34; cf. Acts 2:24, 32). Men's uncovered shaven or short hair and women's covered head and/or long hair serve as a symbol and reminder of women's place under Divine male headship. Paul's God is unequivocally a male God.

A man with long hair or a covered head when praying has disgraced Christ and God. When a woman prays or prophesies with her head uncovered, it is tantamount to shaving her head, and it is a disgrace or indecent (αἰσχρόν). Further, every woman (πᾶσα γυνή) disgraces man (i.e., husband, father, brother, Paul), Christ, and God (11:5). Woman's disgrace is multiplied and has a ripple effect and

16. Oster, "Use, Misuse and Neglect of Archaeological Evidence," 69.

17. Oster, "Use, Misuse and neglect of Archaeological Evidence," 69.

spirals down (or up). What are the ultimate consequences for a woman who *disgraces* or *shames* men and her male God or who transgresses structures and policies maintained by the dominant as forms of control—structures and policies constructed to protect some and punish others, to glorify some and subordinate others based on gender? This language of shame or disgrace is also used at 1 Corinthians 1:27 where the subject is God: God does the shaming, choosing the foolish (μωρά) in the world in order to disgrace (καταισχύνη) the wise (σοφοί) in the world. Paul pits the relative masses among the Corinthian believers (i.e., the many who are *not* wise, powerful, or born into wealthy and/or families of recognized high social position, by human standards) against the few that are considered wise, powerful, and of noble birth by human standards, e.g., Apollos, an eloquent influential Alexandrian apostle who preached in Corinth (1:26, cf. Acts 18:24–28). It is problematic, oppressive, and abusive to build one group's self-worth on the shaming of another group based on known, visible, and/or assumed difference (e.g., religious beliefs, rituals, social class, gender, sexuality, ethnicity, race, clothing, and/or hair texture or style). Often, if not always, what we humans (and Paul *is* human) construct as the foolishness or wisdom of God is nothing more than the foolishness and wisdom of fallible human beings and uninterrogated oppressive and violent normalized human cultural practices.

The shaming of Black girls' hair from outside and within Black communities begins very early and continues through adulthood.[18] Black women and girls are shamed when their hair is considered too kinky or tightly curled; when it is not neatly combed or styled (even young children at play); and when their natural hairstyle is considered too big, too elaborate, a distraction, and/or unprofessional. Dominant others outside of the Black community make policies concerning Black people's hair in public spaces. The fixation with and bias against Black peoples' hair by dominant peoples is a global problem, resulting in emotional, social, and physical trauma to Black girls, women, and men. In the United Kingdom in 2017 a young fourteen-year-old named Ruby Williams was sent home

18. See Richards, "How Black Girl Natural Hair Is Shamed"; Jaima, "American Ignorance"; Mabilishaka, "Don't Get It Twisted."

from school for violating school policy. According to the school's policy at the time (later removed from their website after complaints from the family, which received a £8,500 settlement offer from the London Diocesan Board of Schools, with no admission of the school's liability), Ruby's "afro style hair must be of reasonable size and length."[19] Of course, the dominant nonBlack authorities created and interpreted the racist policy. Ruby asked, "Am I really being sent home because my hair is growing out of my head the way it is?"[20] While preparing and sitting for her General Certificates of Secondary Education (GCSEs) in years 10 and 11, Ruby was repeatedly sent home because of the dominants' discomfort and racial anxieties about her hair and their desire and need to flex their institutional muscles to control this young Black girl through her hair. Understandably, Ruby experienced depression and anxiety about attending school and began seeing a clinical psychologist; the school offered no support. At one point, a teacher attempted to tame Ruby's hair by putting her own hair bands on Ruby's hair. That was too much for Ruby. Frustrated, Ruby responded, "If it's too big can you just please send me home? Because this is not OK." Ruby protested, "Why should I have to cut or change my hair and people can have their hair all the way down to their hips, as long as they want—but because my hair grows out I need to cut it?"[21] Ruby had tried straightening her hair, as well as the time-consuming and costly braids with extensions. Why should a Black child, teen, or adult be forced to alter their hair in order to appear respectable to dominant white society? What is it about Black people's natural hair that frightens or repulses white and/or nonBlack people?

Some Africana people practice a politics of appearance. A "politics of appearance" is "making white people more comfortable with our very presence" and appearance.[22] Some of us truly believe that God has a problem with our hair. We cannot distinguish the voice of God from the voice of Paul. Paul has a lot to do with the

---

19. Virk, "Ruby Williams," 2.

20. Virk, "Ruby Williams," 4.

21. Virk, "Ruby Williams," 6.

22. Byrd and Tharps, *Hair Story*, 4.

way women think about their hair and bodies, about femininity and masculinity, about the spiritual and physical superiority of men over women, and about the male/female binary. Accusations of emasculation of Black men is painfully familiar to Black women. This racialized, gendered society still insists upon a patriarchal binary household structure of which short haired men are the head. As Toni Morrison wrote, "Nothing in black life supports the thesis of black men as feminized by their women and everything points to white male suppression as the emasculating force. Yet this distortion is thriving like health."[23] Often Black women are accused of the feminization and/or emasculation of Black men when they assume leadership roles in the church and society and when they unapologetically excel in the exercise of their talents and gifts in public or domestic spaces.

Internalized hatred of one's hair, skin, and body is sometimes the result of racialized ideologies, policies, and practices targeted at Black women and girls. Black women and girls experience criticism and policing of their hair within the Black community as well. When I attended an African Methodist Episcopal Church in Detroit one Sunday (where I served as an associate minister) with a freshly cut short natural hairstyle, the Black woman senior pastor told me that I looked like a "picaninny." A "picaninny" is a historical racial/racist caricature used for Black children in the U.S.[24] While she meant to shame me, I was shocked and ashamed of her response. She happened to be a dark-skinned African American woman who wore her hair long, bone-straight, and never out of place. Intra-community shaming and abuse that targets women and girls' hair is not limited to African American women and girls.

In other countries and cultures, control of women's and girl's hair and religion intersect so that women and girls who transgress religio-cultural teachings and policies that govern how they must wear and/or cover their hair attracts shaming and violence. On September 13, 2022, Iran's "Morality Police" arrested Mahsa Amini, a twenty-two-year-old woman from Sanandaj in Western Iran. While

23. Morrison, *The Source of Self-Regard*, 93.
24. Pilgrim, "The Picaninny Caricature."

waiting at the Haghani metro stop in Tehran with her brother, the morality police arrested Mahsa for the crime of "improper" hijab (veiling) and took her to the morality police headquarters where she would be forced to participate in an "educational and orientation class." As Mahsa's brother waited for her outside the headquarters, he heard screaming. Two hours later Mahsa was transported to the hospital in a coma, where she died three days later, on September 16. The authorities claimed she suffered cardiac arrest, but women leaving the facility that day said that someone inside had been killed.[25] That was not the first time a woman had been abused while in the custody of the morality police, but Mahsa's death sparked widespread intergenerational protests and defiance in Iran. The authorities have responded with brutal violence and many people have been killed. Firoozeh Kashani-Sabet, an American Iranian historian at the University of Pennsylvania says, "Although we have seen the strangling of women's voices in the past, this extraordinary movement has amplified people's strident cries against political repression in the face of unspeakable peril. The crime that resulted in the unjust and brutal killing of a young woman who was, in fact, very modestly dressed, is nothing short of unconscionable and horrific."[26] Established between 1979 and 1990, Iran's morality police is tasked with making sure that women properly wear the hijab (veil) when in public spaces. The morality police and other male authorities determine whether or not it is being improperly worn (every strand of hair must be concealed). The intentionality of the accused may or may not be a consideration. Women who are out of conformity may be fined and receive up to seventy-four lashes; some have been doused with acid or attacked with knives.[27] Although many Iranian women desire control over their own bodies, it is dominant men who decide when women and girls are out of order and what punishment they deserve when they are determined to have transgressed the morality laws. Ahmed states that women should have a choice, and whatever women decided to

25. Far, "Woman Dies in Custody of Iran's 'Morality Police.'"

26. De Groot, "Iran Protests, Explained."

27. Summers, "The History of Iran's So-Called Morality Police."

do—to wear hijab or not—neither their choices nor their religion should be demonized or criminalized.[28]

Women and Men Who Already Lack
Control over Their Bodies

As stated in chapter 2, first-century Corinth was a Roman colony populated with freedpersons (formerly enslaved, e.g., Chloe), enslaved persons, and the freeborn. The overwhelming majority of enslaved persons in the Corinthian community would not have had husbands or wives and lacked control over their own bodies. The enslaver/slave master is the *head* of the enslaved. Shelly Matthews notes that "sometimes women's heads were shaven against their will, as a deliberate and violent act of shaming associated with accusations of adultery. Furthermore, the forcibly shaven head . . . was a signifier of the shame and degradation of slavery,"[29] especially enslaved women. Would an enslaved woman whose head is forcefully shaven be viewed as transgressing sacralized gender boundaries and thus limited in her participation in the assembly or shunned and shamed? Under Paul's gendered headship rhetoric, an enslaved woman whose hair had been cut off or shaved against her will would have no glory, since, in his view, a woman's long hair is her glory (1 Cor 11:14–15). Paul's head logic and gendered hair salon ethics do not consider women who might lose their hair through an illness or whose hair might grow frail and thin or develop bald patches with age. Illness, stress, and natural aging processes can negatively impact both men and women's hair.

GOD AND NATURE SUPPORT PAUL'S REVISIONIST MYTH OF WOMAN'S SUBORDINATION TO MAN

Men and women who transgress Paul's head logic and salon ethics, reject or oppose Divine order and nature. The man is both

28 See Ahmed, "The Clothes of My Faith"; Saleem, "Shame, Shame."

29. Matthews, "Hearing Wo/men Prophets," 61–62.

the (created) image *and* the glory of God (11:7). But the woman is neither the image nor glory of God; she is the glory of man, since woman derived from man (not directly from God) (11:8). Of course, Genesis 1:26–27 regards the first humans as having been created male and female in God's image. Paul has revised the scriptural witness to suit his cultural ecclesial theo-ideology. He appeals to two creation narratives—the so-called Priestly version in Gen 1:1—2:4a and the Yahwist account in Gen 2:4b—3:24 to support his head logic for the subordination of women to men and the covering of women's heads as symbolic of their acceptance of Paul's theo-ideology. In the Priestly creation story, God created humans, male and female, simultaneously (Gen 1:26, 27); it does not support Paul's head logic.

While Paul argues that neither woman nor man exist independent of one another, he maintains that man was created ahead of the woman and thus is head of the woman (11:11).[30] In oppressive revisionist myths that support the superiority of some peoples over others on the basis of race, ethnicity, gender, class, religion, citizenship, and/or sexual preference (e.g., white Christian nationalism), the reclamation of primordial time is a necessary component to lend authority to the new revised narrative. It is important to make the claim that those considered superior arrived first. Or if those considered superior did not arrive first, but evolved from an inferior first group, they survived (evidence of superiority) and dominated (through violence) as a superior group of people. The revised myth also attributes their survival and dominance through violence to the Divine. Paul claims that all things are from God (11:12); this includes Paul's head logic and most of his teachings in 1 Corinthians.[31]

Finally, Paul invites the Corinthian believers to judge for themselves whether his logic or argument is correct (11:13). Yet, Paul does not rest his case. He argues that nature teaches (disseminates knowledge) that long hair is a dishonor to a man, but a

---

30. Amjad-Ali ("The Equality of Women") argues that Paul is trying to adhere to traditional, cultural symbols that validate the subordination of women to men but transforms the substance.

31. An exception is 1 Corinthians 7:10.

woman's long hair is her glory (11:14, 15; cf. 1 Cor 15:43; 2 Cor 6:8; 11:21; 2 Tim 2:20).[32] In other words, Paul claims that his head logic is *natural*. Practices and ideas that are culturally determined can become so normalized, so rarely contested, that they appear natural, like women's and men's hairstyles, what we eat for breakfast, men as the ideal senior pastors, dominant cisgender white men as the most authoritative interpreters of Scripture, and so on and on.

Similar to Paul, the influential North African early Christian theologian Tertullian (ca. 160–220 CE) a century and a half later in his *De Virginibus Velandis* (*On the Veiling of Virgins*)[33] attempts to maintain collective bodily order that is grounded in a patriarchal interpretation of Scripture, nature, and ecclesiastical discipline.[34] The end result of the persuasive rhetoric of Paul and Tertullian is the (attempted prescriptive) visible veiling or covering of the female body or head. There is power in unobstructed visibility. Such a practice of gendered covering acts as a visible and tangible symbol of a woman's acquiescence to her natural, divine, and ecclesial subordinated status in relation to men, God, and the assembly of believers. Both Paul and Tertullian appeal to a mythical beginning or time of origins, a creative generative moment, and thus they imply that correct individual embodied order means daily (or normalized) re-living or re-membering that mythical beginning in the body (or hair).

32. Elsewhere in the biblical text, men grow their hair long for a period of time, for example, when they are under a vow (Num 6:5; Jdg 16:4–30; Ezek 44:20; cf. Acts 18:18, as Paul himself did). In the apocryphal *Acts of Paul* (Schneemelcher, ed., 238) Titus describes Paul's physical appearance to Onesiphorus of Iconium, who has never met Paul in the flesh. Expecting Paul to arrive in Iconium, Onesiphorus greets him and describes him as "a man small of stature, with a bald head and crooked legs in a good state of body, with eyebrows meeting and nose somewhat hooked, full of friendliness."

33. Tertullian, *Le Voile des Vierges (De Virginibus Verlandis)*.

34. Peters ("Reading 1 Corinthians 11:1–16 through Habits and Hijabs in the United States," 144) argues that Paul rejects "veiling practices derived from the dominant culture's argument on the veiling of women" and thus subverts Roman imperial ideology in favor of "veiling rituals based on Jewish-Christian myth," thereby demonstrating support for persons "less enfranchised by the Roman power structure."

IT'S THE HAIR: TRANSGENDERED PERFORMANCE AND TRANSGRESSIVE FUGITIVITY

Some African peoples participate in cultural-religious ceremonies and rituals that transgress and transgender what others consider normative binary hairstyles for women and men. People in Yoruba culture who consecrate their lives to the gods (the orisa or orisha) undertake extensive preparation, instruction, and a final initiation ceremony that includes shaving the head and painting it with colors and patterns representing the orisha.[35] As with other ethnic groups within Yoruba culture, like the Dada children, parents arrange for the hair to be shaved off their children's heads in a private rite, and "the soothing, cooling, and healing fluid from the snail is rubbed on the head and hair to pacify the deity of Dada children."[36] At other times, Yoruba women will create attractive and embellished and/or simple hairstyles to ensure that their "spiritual head," which is selected prior to birth, "brings good fortune and positive possibilities."[37] The elaborate time-consuming head decorations and hairstyles or "crowning glories" are also created to parade their best appearance.[38] In some Yoruba ceremonies, such as the "Iyawo, 'Wife,'" women's hairstyles are represented in ancestral masquerades that men perform.[39]

While religion, culture, and gender intersect in 1 Corinthians 11, for Black women, men, and children race and sexuality also impact the violence perpetrated against them when they choose to wear natural and/or nonbinary hairstyles. In general, the melanin present and apparent in the skin of Africana peoples reveals Africana ancestry in the racialized society of the U.S.A. Even if the melanin in one's skin is insufficient to determine conclusively whether one is Black or white (i.e., one can pass for white), historically the white dominant society has relied on knowledge or rumor

35. Drewal, "Crowning Glories," 230.

36. Drewal, "Crowning Glories," 227.

37. Drewal, "Crowning Glories," 229.

38. Drewel, "Crowning Glories," 229–30.

39. Drewel, "Crowning Glories," 235.

about one's African-descended kinfolk to determine racial identity in the case of people who could pass as white. Historically, a person determined or rumored to have one drop of Black blood was considered Black. Some Black persons who looked white attempted to pass as white in order to obtain the freedoms, rights, and privileges of being white. We see this played out in cinematic renditions of the story of the "tragic mulatto," e.g., *Imitation of Life* and *Passing*.[40] The "tragic mulatto" was a fugitive from blackness who attempted to transgress the ideologically and socially constructed boundaries of blackness and whiteness and its material implications.

But other Black peoples enslaved in the U.S.A. attempted to pass for white, temporarily, with no intention of living as a white person indefinitely. Such persons strove to pass, run, or ride into freedom where enslavement had been declared illegal. Historically, Black transgressive and transgendering behaviors have been for the purpose of liberation from white enslavement. When Ellen and William Craft strategized their escape to freedom, they transformed Ellen into a white man, since her very light skin color made it possible for her to pass as white. In their narrative *Running a Thousand Miles for Freedom*, William writes the following:

> Just before the time arrived, in the morning, for us to leave, I cut off my wife's hair square at the back of the head and got her to dress in the disguise and stand out on the floor. I found that she made a most respectable looking gentleman. My wife had no ambition whatever to assume this disguise, and would not have done so had it been possible to have obtained our liberty by more simple means; but we knew it was not customary in the South for ladies to travel with male servants; and therefore, notwithstanding my wife's fair complexion, it would

40. There are two versions of the classic film the *Imitation of Life*, one released in 1934 and a second in 1959. The film *Passing* is based on Nella Larsen's 1929 novel *Passing*, which is a 2021 black-and-white romantic drama film written, produced, and directed by Rebecca Hall. It follows the unexpected reunion of two Black women who were high school friends (one of whom is passing as white and is married to an unwitting white man), whose rekindled acquaintance ignites a mutual obsession that threatens both of their carefully constructed realities.

have been a very difficult task for her to have come off as a free white lady, with me as her slave; . . . in Georgia (and I believe in all the slave States [*sic*]) every coloured person's complexion is *prima facie* evidence of his being a slave.[41]

Black women and men have had to assimilate and/or transform their natural hair (or shave it off in the case of Ellen Craft) in order to survive as fugitives running toward freedom, pre-and post-emancipation. William and Ellen Craft identified as God-believing Christians, but they condemn the Christianity of the cruel enslavers. Craft wrote, "My old master had the reputation of being a very humane and Christian man, but he thought nothing of selling my poor old father, and my dear aged mother [and later William's brother and sister], at separate times, to different persons, to be dragged off never to behold each other again, til summoned to appear before the great tribunal of heaven. . . . This shameful conduct gave me a thorough hatred, not for true Christianity, but for slaveholding piety."[42] In fugitivity and on their way to freedom, the Crafts transgressed the gendered mandate that women wear long hair, and they did so in order to cross into freedom. Black women, men, and children continue to transgress and transgender the glass ceilings erected on their bodies and heads in the quest for unmitigated freedom, to exist unapologetically as fully embodied persons of African descent. In *Black on Both Sides: A Racial History of Trans Identity* C. Riley Snorton writes that early Black fugitives

41. Craft, *Running a Thousand Miles*, 700–701. William thought of the plan and disguise and suggested it to Ellen. She had first considered it impossible for her to carry on the pretense for a thousand miles through slave states. "However, on the other hand, she also thought of her condition. She saw that the laws under which we lived did not recognize her to be a woman, but a mere chattel, to be bought and sold, or otherwise dealt with as her owner might see fit. Therefore the more she contemplated her helpless condition, the more anxious she was to escape from it. She said, 'I think it is almost too much for us to undertake; however, I feel that God is on our side, and with his assistance, notwithstanding all the difficulties, we shall be able to succeed. Therefore, if you will purchase the disguise, I will try to carry out the plan'" (697). Ellen also had to speak the derogatory racial language of white enslavers as they ran toward freedom, traversing by train (e.g., 717–18).

42. Craft, *Running a Thousand Miles*, 686.

seeking freedom passed in terms of gender and race; Black women passed as white men. Their skin was sufficiently light and their hair appropriately straight for them to pass as white without arousing suspicion, at least in the short term and sometimes for life.[43] Black people's hair texture is considered the most telling feature of blackness. When light-skinned Black people tried to pass for white to escape racial hatred and violence, if the hair "showed just a little bit of kinkiness, they would be unable to pass as White. . . . Hair acted as the true test of Blackness, which is why some male slaves shaved their heads . . . when attempting to escape to freedom."[44]

HANDS OFF OUR HAIR

Black women, men, and children struggle with dominant white people's and even nonBlack people of color's anxiety and curiosity about their hair, many of whom cannot resist the temptation to touch, critique, or even abuse Black peoples hair, without their permission and act as if petting some exotic domesticated creature. More disturbing, the loose, braided, fro'd and loc'd hair of Black children has been cut off without their parents' permission and against the child's will in public, at wrestling matches, in classrooms, and on school buses.

Most Black girls experience white people's and some people of color's exoticization of their hair, an odd fascination and othering, as early as pre-school or elementary school. I remember little white girls touching my long black braids, without my permission, in the bathroom in elementary school and being surprised at how soft it was. Softness was not generally associated with curly or ultra-curly hair, not because it was not soft, but because in the white cultural imagination and construction of blackness, nothing about Black people was human or soft. Femininity in the white cultural imagination, often adopted or assimilated to by people of color with straight hair and many Black people, is associated with long, soft, straight hair.

43. Snorton, *Black on Both Sides*.

44. Byrd and Tharps, *Hair Story*, 17.

Janet Jackson shared in her 2022 Lifetime docuseries that when she and her family moved from Gary, Indiana, to a white neighborhood and school system in California, one of her earliest memories was of white children touching her hair because it was different from theirs and rubbing her skin, asking "does that come off."[45] Most black women have similar stories of white persons and people of color touching our hair without our permission. It starts for us as children and follows us into adulthood. This unwanted, uninvited touching of my hair was done to me just a few years ago while in Bangalore, India—the objectification of my body, my person, through my hair. If I had not been in a group listening to a poor Dalit woman share her story with my back turned to some of my colleagues when two of them put their hands in my hair, I might have said, "Please, take your hands off my hair." But I did not, so as not to disrupt the woman's story. I don't know what each expected to discover from touching my hair. During that same gathering, a black male colleague asked if I planned to let my hair grow long, as if there was something wrong with my short natural hair.

Black women, men, and children have been told that their natural hair is unbecoming, unprofessional, and unkempt by white people and by Black and Brown people who have internalized racism and assimilated to white beauty standards. In 2019, California passed the CROWN ("Creating a Respectful and Open World for Natural Hair") Act. It is an attempt to recognize that many African Americans are subject to discrimination based on Eurocentric expectations of beauty and professionalism. Black men and women have suffered discrimination in California and across the U.S.A. and beyond that relates to their natural hair and the hairstyles they use to protect their natural hair. The CROWN Act recognizes that our nation has long equated "Blackness" and characteristics associated with Blackness as evidence of inferiority. This supposed inferiority has allowed Black people to be treated unequally based on their natural characteristics.[46]

45. Jackson, "Janet Jackson."
46. Hamilton, "Untangling Discrimination."

Some Black women will go to great lengths to assimilate and appear professional by white dominant standards. When I was in my doctoral program, a Black woman in the master's program confided that she had very little money and had to choose between buying groceries and getting her hair done. Someone she trusted advised her to spend the little money she had at the beauty salon getting her hair done (in this case it was quite costly because it involved redoing a hair weave) and then find a food bank for groceries. While I was somewhat shocked by the advice and her choice to follow it, I also understand the pressure on Black women in churches and society to present themselves as professional-looking at all times, which can be costly. Yet middle-class Black women are too often critical of poor Black women who yield to the same pressure but with less money. If Black women, men, and children (and others) can be convinced that something innate, natural to their being, something they are born with, is a sign of their inferiority, of their subordinate status, they will wage war against their own bodies and the bodies of other Black people.

BREAKING THE INTRACTABLE GLASS
CEILING ERECTED ON OUR HEADS

Black women and girls in general, in different and various ways, have been taught that their hair is more important than any other part of their bodies and should conform to white beauty standards; the straighter (and longer) the better. Thus, Black women chemically straighten their hair (which has been proven to negative impact women's health) and/or purchase weaves or wigs to hide their natural hair. Black women who opt for twa's are often suspect in terms of transgressing gender and sexual binaries and heteronormative ideas about sexuality; they are viewed as militant and not easily controlled.

Black people are not without good reasons for assimilating to white beauty standards when it "is a key determinant in economic success and social advancement. . . . Since slavery, whites have rewarded blacks for looking almost white."[47] We have been taught that our hair is only our friend when we can make it conform to a certain standard or image. When it is in "disarray" or "out of order," it must be tamed; it is our friend only if we tame it. And to allow our hair to be disorderly or wild in public is the ultimate taboo. When African American gymnast Gabby Douglas's hair did not conform to some Black women's expectations *while* she was participating in the Olympics, she drew the ire and insults of too many Black women who called her hair "unkempt" and "embarrassing." But Gabby had the appropriate response, which echoed her mom's statements when interviewed by the Associated Press: "I just made history and people are focused on my hair? It can be bald or short; it doesn't matter about [my] hair."[48] While Gabby may have broken the glass ceiling as a gold and silver medal winner in the 2012 and 2016 Olympics, too many tried to hold intact the ceiling erected over her head or hair. Alice Walker wrote that following about her journey lifting the ceiling off the top of her brain:

> Not my friend hair itself, for I quickly understood that it was innocent. It was the way I related to it that was the problem. I was always thinking about it. So much so that if my spirit had been a balloon eager to soar away and merge with the infinite, my hair would be the rock that anchored it to Earth. I realized that there was no hope of continuing my spiritual development, no hope of future growth of my soul, no hope of really being able to stare at the universe and forget myself entirely in the staring (one of the purest joys!) if I still remained chained to thoughts about my hair. I suddenly understood why nuns and monks shaved their heads! . . . Eventually I knew precisely what hair wanted: it wanted to grow, to be itself, to attract lint, if that was its destiny, but to be left alone by anyone, including me, who did not love it as it was. What do you think happened? . . . The ceiling at the top of my brain lifted; once again my mind (and spirit) could get outside myself. I would not be stuck in

47. Kaba, "When Black Hair Tangles with White Power," 105.

48. Eugenios, "Gabby Douglas' Mom Weighs in on Hair Controversy." See also Wilson, "Haters Attack Gabby Douglas' Hair Again."

restless stillness but would continue to grow. The plant
was above ground! This was the gift of my growth during
my fortieth year.[49]

Many churched (and unchurched) women have been con-
vinced that their hair is their glory. In the scheme of things, glorified
hair is long and straight. Long straight hair represents well-coiffured
tresses and the height of femininity and is a girl or woman's ticket
to male (and female) respectability, the coveted boyfriend or husband, a good job, and the respectability of other women and society
as a whole. Given this fetish and obsession around women's long
straight hair that is equated with divine femininity, Black women's
natural hair is constructed as the antithesis of femininity and as further evidence of Black women's inferiority and absolute difference.

PAUL WILL NOT SILENCE US! WE WILL BREAK THROUGH!

In 1 Corinthians 11:1–16, Paul objectifies women's bodies through
their hair to create patriarchal order within the assemblies of believers in ancient first-century Corinth. Order that diminishes bodily
autonomy is violent and oppressive, especially when it attempts to
do so by convincing women that their bodies are inherently inferior
to men's bodies. Paul requests his target audience to view themselves—their gifts, talents, passions—within a limited framework.
Paul must first, however, claim his own authority to order, name,
and limit their speech, bodies, and gifts. He claims authority when
he asserts that he imitates Christ and therefore the Corinthians
should imitate him, which implies and assumes that Paul knows
and has a better understanding than others of what Christ desires
of his followers. Paul was among those who had the privilege of
communicating with the resurrected Christ, and none were women
(ch. 15). Any claim to know the mind of the risen Christ is already
gendered male. Thus, women's claims to authority are already
subordinated to Paul, if authority is constructed on the basis of to

49. Walker, "Oppressed Hair Puts a Ceiling on the Brain," 285–86, 287.

whom the risen Christ appeared. Paul has declared himself Christ's proxy among the Corinthian believers.

Paul's rhetoric, his head logic, enlists women to participate in their own subordination and silencing and in the policing, control, and muting of each another. Paul's arguments in 1 Corinthians 11 cannot be read in isolation from the rest of the letter. Many scholars argue that Paul's explicit command that women should be silent in the religious assemblies is an interpolation (14:33, 34).[50] But Paul's attempt to silence or subordinate women in chapter 14 is continuous with Paul's efforts to subordinate and regulate women's speech and bodies in 1 Corinthians 11. Jill Marshall argues convincingly that chapters 11–14 are interrelated and reflect Paul's ambivalence about women's speech, a vacillation that resembles other authors roughly contemporary with Paul (i.e., Livy, Philo, and Plutarch). Further, Marshall asserts the following:

> In 1 Corinthians 11–14, Paul modifies his recommenda-
> tions about whether and how women should speak in the
> assembly. Issues about the spaces and definitions of the
> ἐκκλησία, religious experiences, gender difference and
> hierarchy, and shame surface throughout the arguments
> in 1 Corinthians 11–14 and strain Paul's ambivalence to-
> wards women's speech, evident in 1 Cor 11:2–16, to the
> point where he instructs against their speaking at all.[51]

As a womanist talking back to and throwing shade on Paul, I say, "Take your hands out of my hair!" I am a human being equal to all other human beings across gender, sexuality, race, class, citizenship, and religion. The length (or texture) of my hair, covered or uncovered, is only a symbol of my relationship to God and Christ if *I choose to make it one*; not because you say so, Paul. I dissent from your head logic, Paul, that my hair is a visible sign of my subordinated status. Take your hands out of my hair, Paul! Leave my hair alone, Paul. I am not my hair. My hair is part of me. But I am not my hair. I Protest!

50. See, e.g., Lavrinovica, "Syntactic Flexibility"; Wilson, "Recasting Paul as a Chauvinist."

51. Marshall, *Women Praying and Prophesying in Corinth*, 107–8.

POETIC PROTEST: I AM THE GLORY OF MY HAIR!

So, Paul says I, a woman, have no glory
Glory of my own, without a man
That man is my glory
And my covered or long hair testifies so
Says Paul
Let me, "Get this twisted,"
I do protest
Talk back to Paul
Interrogate him, even reject
Paul's Patriarchal Kephalogic
His noggin-logic
Framed as Christocentric God-Talk
All God-Talk is cultural and fallible human talk
Paul's God-Talk is no exception
Talkin' 'bout four heads above mine
God, Jesus, Paul, and other men
Man, Paul says, is the head of woman
And the head is woman's glory
Glory of men, of Paul, of Christ, of God!
Paul's God is a patriarchal Man
Unreformed Man
For whom Paul speaks
Still, I dissent!
I testify otherwise
I am the Glory of Mother God
My hair is not my glory
It is not the glass ceiling
Paul attempts to erect my head
I reject
Paul's God-talk, his patriarchal 'ligion
About my head, my hair, or that veil
He wants me to hide under
Muffling my prayers and oracles
Like Nancy Ambrose
I take issue with Paul

Hands Off Our Hair, Paul!

He is not *the* voice of God
God speaks to me too, to us women
Black women too
It's true
Some of Us will bend our backs
Our sisters' backs
To avoid pissing Paul's God off!
To avoid cracking the ceiling Paul erected
On our heads, on our bodies
But, as for me, I dissent
I did not ask Paul for
Advice on how to wear or style my hair
So don't touch my hair
Leave my hair alone!
Get your hands out of my hair, Paul!
My hair is not for your glory!
Neither is it my glory!
I am, all of me, the crowning act of God's glory
All of me, regardless of
What my hair decides to do
Or what I do with or to my hair
God did not tame my hair
And neither shall you
I am God's creation and not man's
From head to toe
I cannot, will not be reduced
To Paul's assessment of women
Of my body, my head, my hair
Or my skin
All of me is divine
From the crown of my independent,
doing their own thing
Strong-willed
Strands of hair
That refuse to be restrained
No part of me was
Created to be subdued

By other folks' God-talk about me
Even in the Bible
Oppressive God-talk
About my hair and skin,
Glorious skin and hair
A head of hair to be tamed
I will not be controlled or shamed
by theo-ideologies in sacred texts
About me and my hair
My thick, thin, sparse, liberated strands
My long, short, shaven, falling or standing tall hair
Is a part of me
I will not deny
I will not hide under
A veil of inferiority
And I will not pawn
For a ring and a white dress with a veil
Not under the covering you constructed for me
I will let it be
let my hair be
If I choose
Or I will trim, big chop,
shave or let it grow into long gorgeous locs
And if or when I do shave, cover, or loc my hair
I won't be shamed
Into hiding my coils
Because you insist
That my God-given strands
Are a symbol of my inferiority
Or a reminder of your fears
Of me, and my people
Nothing about me
Is inferior
I am not who you say I am
If it is less than I am
I am not my hair
But my hair is part of me

A glorious part of me
But don't get it twist
It is I
I am God's crowning glory
All of me is organically glorious
My hair is not the sole witness
Testifying to who I am
My hair is a testament, a visible image
Of the complexity of my existence in this world,
Of my resilience and flexibility,
My independence and how I am intwined with others
Of how the divine has sculpted me,
Over and over into a creation of beautiful diversity
I am more than my beautifully crafted hair
Oh, so much more.
I am glorious in God's sight
All of me!
Asé!

CHAPTER 5

Paul's Sexual Politics and Black Women's Contested Love

Reclaiming Hope and the Necessity of Self-Love[1]

"Utilizing a more liberal interpretation acknowledges that biblical restrictions on premarital sex often involve a totalizing view of sexuality that is lust-based and not expressed in loving, monogamous relationships."

MONIQUE MOULTRIE[2]

"Were you never in love with anyone, a pretty girl, or pretty boy, a slave, a freedman?—What, then, has that to do with being either slave or free? Were you never commanded by your sweetheart to do something you didn't wish to do? . . . What else, then, is slavery?"

EPICTETUS, PHILOSOPHER AND FREEDMAN OF EPAPHRODITUS (FREEDMAN AND SECRETARY OF THE ROMAN EMPEROR NERO)[3]

---

1. This chapter is a significantly revised version of my essay "'Loves Never Fails,'" in Sirvent and Reyburn, *Theologies of Failure*.

2. Moultrie, "Interrogating the Passionate and the Pious," 114. See also Moultrie, *Passionate and Pious*.

3. Oldfather, *Epictetus*, Book IV.I.16–17 (p. 249).

"Love forever lingers; it accommodates everyone and everything, but herself. Love expects little for herself; she boasts of no accomplishments and is never proud. Love is never disrespectful, even when silenced and abused. She makes no demands and has no dreams. Love has no reason to be resentful or irritable, her man has been good to her; she could do worse. Love does not delight in opposing injustice or in her oppressor's destruction; she is content with the reasons for her subjugation. Love bears all things, believes all things, and interrogates none. Love expresses no hope for her own needs and desires; she endures everything with a smile. Such love will never be freed without a fight. . . . Before I knew better, I spoke like a child of my oppressor; I thought like my abuser; I imitated them. When I recognized my shackles, I broke free, I rejected a self-less love. . . . Now three—faith, hope, and love—survive, but what I now need most is hope, hope that envisions something better, the not yet seen, the yet to be, the can be, and will be, a different love that respects her body, voice, choices, dreams, desires (sexual and nonsexual), gifts, and achievements."

1 Cor 13:4–8a, 11, 13 remixed,
Mitzi J. Smith

Renita Weems observes that the Song of Solomon is "eight chapters teeming with lust, love, sex, and passion in the middle of the Bible— and not once does the heroine or her beloved talk about marriage as a way to seal their love and as the institution in which they might properly express their pent-up sexual frustration."[4] Most Christians do not base their sexual ethics on the Song of Solomon but on the sexual advice of the apostle Paul, who might just be asexual. To be fair, Pauline sexual ethics as articulated in 1 Corinthians 7 discourages marriage because of an impending crisis. In the context of that crisis, sexual relations between men and women function as a mechanism for managing lust, maintaining self-control, and refraining from sexual immorality (πορνεία). Perhaps many con- temporary readers who negotiate relationships in the context of

---

4. Weems, *What Matters Most*, 17.

perennial and intersecting crises (i.e., racism, sexism, queerphobia, classism, poverty, misogynoir, illness, pandemics, and/or seasonal hormonal upheaval during puberty and menopause) understand and empathize with Paul's concerns and response in 1 Corinthians 7. Paul offers significant advice about self-control, lust/desire (but not natural sexual attraction), obligatory sexual relations, sexual immorality, and marriage, which in many cases exceeds what most modern Christian readers receive in their homes, churches, synagogues, temples, or mosques. Discussion of sex (and sexuality), in those spaces, is rare, more often than not. And so, for too many Christian readers, Paul's sexual ethics may, by default, be the standard.

This chapter discusses the sexual politics and ethics that Paul rhetorically constructs and advocates that men and women among the Corinthian believers should embrace and practice. And his sexual politics and ethics have nothing to do with love and do not insist on marriage, given the crisis that confronts them. Five chapters separate the Pauline sexual ethics of chapter 7 and Paul's prescriptive characterization of love in chapter 13 of 1 Corinthians. The language of God's/the Spirit's gift (χάρισμα, 7:7; 12:27—14:1) links the two chapters. Paul is exempt from his own sexual ethics because of God's gift to him: "I wish that all were as I myself am. But each has a particular gift from God" (7:7 NRSV). In 1 Corinthians 12:37—14:1, the Spirit's gifts should be exercised in love; otherwise, they will be ineffective or impotent. Paul's rhetoric in chapters 7 and 13 of 1 Corinthians will be examined in conversation with Black women and men's contested struggles for love—to love when, how, and whom they choose—in enslavement and freedom.

In *Black Women, Black Love,* Dianne Stewart asserts that in March 1865 in the post-enslavement U.S. South, the Freedmen's Bureau directed the reconstruction of the Southern social institution of patriarchal marriage among the formerly enslaved and poor white people. The Bureau's representatives "were assigned responsibility for marrying Black couples and influencing them to embrace monogamy and the gender roles expected of wives and husbands. In effect, the government sought to prepare postenslaved African descendants for compliant citizenship through the institutions of heterosexual marriage and the patriarchal family."[5] This federal social program commenced a new stage of "America's long history of interference with Black love" since enslavement.[6] Enslaved Black men and women were not generally permitted to enter into legal marriages. In the process of forcing newly freed slaves to register their marriages, federal authorities dissolved "intricate polygamous unions slavery had designed for a great number of African Americans," forcing them into monogamous marriage to the detriment of Black women and their children.[7] Black men were married to the wife with the greatest number of children, so that those children would not become the responsibility of the Bureau. The other wives were abandoned to raise, for example, their two or three children alone.

When Black enslaved persons that were separate from "husbands" and "wives" during enslavement located their partners and found that they had remarried, they were legally prosecuted and penalized for bigamy. Additionally, judges ordered the removal of Black children from their families and placed them with their former enslavers under the pretense of altruistic care, but the goal was to provide former enslavers with a pool of free labor. This practice continued for two years after emancipation until the Supreme Court stopped it in 1867.[8]

PAULINE SEXUAL POLITICS AND ETHICS: LUST, SELF-CONTROL, SEXUAL IMMORALITY, MONOGAMY, AND MARRIAGE

Marriage is not a priority for Paul, at least not in his current context, but the prevention and curbing of sexual immorality is crucial. Paul agrees with the Corinthian believers' statement that "it is good for a man to keep his hands off a woman," if touching leads to sexual immorality (1 Cor 7:1). But which man? Which woman? The man's

---

5. Stewart, *Black Women, Black Love*, 63.

6. Stewart, *Black Women, Black Love*, 62.

7. Stewart, *Black Women, Black Love*, 64.

8. Stewart, *Black Women, Black Love*, 69.

identity and his relationship to the woman are not stated. Is the man her stepson (as in 1 Cor 5:1)? Is he her father, enslaver/slave master, or brother? Is he a man with access to more than one woman, e.g., an enslaver and/or a wealthy and/or noble man? I argue that in his response, Paul assumes a relationship between an unmarried man and an unmarried woman *and* recommends monogamy as a means to manage lust and prevent further sexual immorality in the community (1 Cor 7:1–7), like the case of the believer who is cohabitating with his stepmother (his father's wife) (1 Cor 5:1–13). The problem is not that they are cohabitating but that the woman is already married, it seems, and to her lover's father. According to Paul, not even pagans tolerate that kind of sexual immorality. All sexual immorality is intolerable and detrimental to the entire community; violators must be identified as wicked and ostracized, as if to prevent contagion and a pandemic.

In order to avoid sexual immorality (διὰ πορνείας), each man should have his own woman, and each woman, her own man (7:2). In 1 Corinthians 7:2–7, dominant translators render the Greek words ἀνήρ (man) and γυνή (woman) as husband and wife, respectively. However, I propose that Paul is not urging the Corinthian men who believe it is not good for a man to touch a woman to get married. The language of marriage (γάμος, ἀγάμος), which Paul is not shy about using in chapter 7, is absent from the rhetoric of verses 7:2–7. Paul is proposing monogamous committed relationships between men and women that guard against sexual immorality (e.g., adulterous sexual relationships with already married persons and/or with relatives, or with persons engaged in prostitution). For men and women who desire/lust for each other, they should satisfy their desires/lusts within monogamous relationships. In Paul's logic, there seems to be no such thing as natural sexual attraction, sexual attraction that is not lust, or does not become lust. Paul does not mention or recommend marriage for men who fear the consequences of touching a woman. In fact, Paul is not a fan of marriage for anyone in the imminent crisis (7:26), not for the unmarried/single, widows, engaged virgins, or engaged men, particularly if they can otherwise practice self-control and avoid sexual immorality (1 Cor 7:8–9, 25–26, 32, 36, 40). Within the monogamous relationship, the man and woman each are commanded to render to each other what lust demands, which is satisfaction through sexual intercourse (τὴν ὀφειλὴν ἀποδιδότω, 7:3). For the man exercises authority over the woman's body and likewise the woman exercises control over the man's body (7:4). They are mutually accountable. For only one reason (i.e., an intimate two-person prayer meeting?) should monogamous couples withhold sexual intercourse from one another, otherwise Satan will take advantage of their lack of control (ἀκρασίαν, 7:5). Both men and women lack self-control when it comes to sexual lust. Paul has in mind the overwhelming power of lust/desire in heterosexual relationships. Paul's sexual ethics excludes relationships outside of a normalized gender binary and only recognizes heterosexual relationships. Queering community boundaries marked by sexual immorality, Midori Hartman argues that Paul attempts to squash divisions "in favor of a limited range of approved and status quo-informed ways of being in and in relation to the body of Christ"; thus, the assembly of believers must police "its boundaries against *porneia*" as Paul defines it.[9]

For the apostle Paul, sexual relationships within committed monogamous relationships or in marriage are not about pleasure; they are for the purpose of managing lust/desire, demonstrating mutual control, and avoiding sexual immorality. Michael Brown asserts that "sex for pleasure or satisfaction (i.e., desire) was considered illegitimate because it demonstrated a lack . . . of self-control. Furthermore, homosexual sexual practice was dismissed because it questioned an implicit vision of masculinity that the church never challenged."[10]

Ideally, Paul wishes everybody could be like him to whom God has given a gift (1 Cor 7:7, 40). It is not clear what that gift is. Is Paul asexual or queer? Is he impotent? Has he never lusted for a woman? Is God's gift the mastery or self-control of his own body and desires/lust? Has an unsuccessful marriage cured him of the desire for a relationship? It is impossible to know for certain the nature of Paul's gift.

9. Hartman, "A Little *Porneia* Leavens the Whole," 158.

10. Brown, "An Inconsistent Truth," 61. See also Best, "Everybody Knew He Was 'That Way.'"

Paul's rule in all the assemblies of believers is that everyone should remain as they were when God called them (even unmarried?); they should not seek to change their material condition or social status (1 Cor 7:17–24). It is instructive that the two examples Paul deploys to support this universal teaching are circumcision and enslavement. Circumcision, of course, is ordinarily performed on eight-day-old male infants and sometimes on grown men (e.g., Timothy, Acts 16:1–5); once done, it cannot be undone. At first thought, circumcision and enslavement seem a strange pairing. However, circumcision could in this case function as a referent for enslavement, so that circumcision and enslavement are parallel examples. Hector Avalos argued convincingly that circumcision could be viewed as a slave mark.[11] A person who is enslaved when God called her, cannot free herself. She cannot undo her enslavement. Only her enslaver can agree to set her free. The power of manumission or emancipation is entirely in the hands of her master. Sheila Briggs, Jennifer Glancy, and Shelly Matthews have raised questions about the impact of Paul's teaching on enslaved persons.[12] Paul knew, of course, that enslaved persons have no control over their own sexuality or bodies and could not marry without their master's/enslavers consent. If it is the enslaver, freeborn, and freedperson who assert that "it is not good for a man to touch a woman," perhaps in their new lives as believers they are now concerned about the authority they have over and access to the bodies of enslaved women for whom they lust or desire sexually. Enslavers possess absolute control over the bodies (sexually or non-sexually), time, children, labor, potential, gifts, and speech of their human property. It is generally unacceptable or frowned upon for enslavers to marry enslaved persons. And enslavers/masters seldom permit their enslaved persons to marry.

Paul, not the Lord, advises that believing and nonbelieving men and women remain in their relationships, if at all possible.

11. Avalos, "Circumcision as a Slave Mark." Catherine Hezser (*Jewish Slavery in Antiquity*, 31) asserts that circumcision of enslaved persons should not be regarded "as a conversion rite, since the circumcised slave did not become a proselyte."

12. Glancy, *Slavery in Early Christianity*, 39–70; Briggs, "Paul on Bondage and Freedom"; and Matthews, "Hearing Wo/men Prophets," 60–61.

Here again, Paul does not use the language of marriage, as he does elsewhere in chapter 7. In light of the impending crisis, Paul does not favor marriage unless one is already married (7:26). The believing man who is in a relationship with a nonbelieving woman can live with her in a monogamous committed relationship, if she consents to the arrangement (1 Cor 7:12–13). The believer makes the unbeliever holy and any children born to them are holy and not unclean (1 Cor 7:14). If the unbeliever leaves the home and thus the committed relationship, so be it, for what is important is peace (1 Cor 7:15). The hope is that the unbelieving partner might save (as in bring peace to him, her, or them?) the unbelieving one (1 Cor 7:16). Love has no place in Paul's sexual ethics. Perhaps what we see in Paul's advice in chapter 7 is the influence of Greek philosophical teaching about self-control and freedom.

The ancient philosopher Epictetus was born into enslavement; his mother was enslaved. Enslavement is meant to be an inhuman existence void of love. Epictetus was enslaved during the reign of the Roman Emperor Nero (54–68 CE). As an enslaved man belonging to Epaphroditus, Epictetus had the privilege of learning philosophy from the Roman philosopher Gaius Musonius Rufus (25–95 CE; exiled from Rome in 65 CE). This opportunity allowed Epictetus himself to become a philosopher in freedom, but it did not lighten the violence of his enslavement. His master could flog him at any time for any reason. One of Epictetus's legs was permanently damaged from physical abuse suffered during his enslavement.[13] As a freedman, Epictetus was passionate about freedom and its true meaning. He taught that a man who lacks self-control in any area of life is no different from an enslaved person. In fact, such a man is enslaved to anything and everyone that can compel him to do what he does not desire to do. Epictetus considered love to be the enemy of self-control and thus an obstruction to the achievement of absolute freedom:

> Tell the truth, then, slave, and do not run away from your masters, nor make denial, nor dare to present your emancipator, when you have so many proofs to convict

---

13. Bradley, *Slavery and Society at Rome*, 175.

you of slavery. And, indeed, when a man out of passionate love is under the compulsion to do something contrary to his opinion, all the time seeing the better thing
but lacking the strength to follow, one might be all the
more inclined to regard him as deserving pity, because
he is in the grip of something violent, and, in a manner
of speaking, divine.[14]

According to Epictetus, one must destroy the power that
passion or desire has over one's life: "For freedom (ἐλευθερία)
is not acquired by satisfying yourself with what you desire (τῶν
ἐπιθυμουμένων) but destroying your desire (τῆς ἐπιθυμίας)."[15] The
apostle Paul, of course, is not concerned with freedom but with the
avoidance of sexual immorality through the mutual satisfaction of
sexual desire within committed relationships. Such relationships,
according to Pauline sexual ethics, function to conquer or control
lust.

For Epictetus, to be truly free, one must be loosely tied to everything and everyone, including wives and children.[16] Diogenes,
according to Epictetus, was a truly free man because "everything he
had was easily loosed, everything was merely tied on, . . . [including
his property, limbs, body, kinfolk, friends, and country]. . . . His
true ancestors, indeed, the gods, and his real Country, he would
never have abandoned, nor would he have suffered another to yield
them more obedience and submission. . . ."[17] The truly free person
is not compelled by another person or thing outside of himself to
do anything, not even the love of another human being.[18] God is the
Giver by whom no human can avoid being compelled.

In Paul's sexual ethics in chapter 7 of 1 Corinthians, love is not
a factor. As with Epictetus, love has nothing to do with it; it is about

14. Oldfather, *Epictetus*, Book IV.I.146–47 (p. 295).

15. Oldfather, *Epictetus*, Book IV.I.175 (p. 305).

16. Oldfather, *Epictetus*, Book IV.I.159 (p. 299). Epictetus never achieved
the freedom about which he taught; he was "not yet able to look into the face
of my masters. I still honour [*sic*] my paltry body, I take great pains to keep it
sound, although it is not sound in any case" (IV.I.151 [p. 297]).

17. Oldfather, *Epictetus*, Book IV.I.153–55 (p. 297).

18. Oldfather, *Epictetus*, Book IV.I.36, 146–47 (p. 295).

self-control and the avoidance of sexual immorality. And, of course, it is Paul, informed by his own cultural context, who determines what constitutes sexual immorality. Brown asserts that Paul demonstrates "a complicated relationship to the institution of marriage based on whether or not the believer has the spiritual gift of self-control."[19] The language of God's gift to Paul in chapter 7 provides a link to his characterization of love in chapter 13 where the gifts of God's Spirit should function in love.

WHAT'S LOVE GOT TO DO WITH IT?

Monique Moultrie argues that "a womanist sexual ethics posits that healthy intimate relationships can exist without leading to or requiring marriage, and that marriage is not the only indicator of relational success."[20] Neither Pauline sexual ethics, in the context of crisis, nor Moultrie's womanist sexual ethics consider marriage as necessary or expedient. But Pauline monogamy is loveless. In the century after emancipation, Black love struggled to survive the trauma enslavement and the slow and gradual violence of oppressive U.S. laws, policies, and initiatives; the terror of lynching; race riots that targeted Black communities and flourishing; white American patriarchy; an inhumane welfare system; the blaming and shaming of Black mothers; the "war on drugs" and the building of the contemporary prison industrial complex; and disproportionate evictions of Black women and their children.[21] The respectability politics of patriarchal marriage did not save or shield Black love from the multifarious assaults against it.

Monogamous committed sexual relationships between men and women, within or outside of marriage in chapter 7 and Paul's characterization of love in chapter 13 serve as mechanisms of control and prevention. Love limits and guards against the ineffective and impotent exercise of gifts (1 Cor 13:1–3). Love is not required for a moral and ethical monogamous relationship between a man

---

19. Brown, "An Inconsistent Truth," 55.

20. Moultrie, "Interrogating the Passionate and the Pious," 115.

21. Stewart, *Black Women, Black Love*, 92, 101; chapter 4.

and a woman or inside or outside of marriage, but what is required is self-control and mutual commitment to satisfy sexual desires/lust. The ultimate goal is the avoidance of sexual immorality through self-control and mutuality, which is achieved in committed relationships in which each party satisfies the sexual desires/lust of the other.

THE LIMITS OF PAULINE LOVE

The love that Paul defines in chapter 13 must be understood in the context of the gendered patriarchal hierarchy that Paul constructs elsewhere in 1 Corinthians.[22] Chapter 13 is sandwiched between Paul's chapter 12 on spiritual gifts and chapter 14 regulating the gift of prophecy and the use of gifts in worship, including the subordination and silencing of women. Paul's teaching about love (in relationship to spiritual gifts) cannot be read in isolation from the rhetorical and ideological subordination of women to men in 1 Corinthians 11:2–16. Paul constructs a prescriptive definition of love that should temper the arrogant and boastful use of spiritual gifts, perhaps especially the gifts of praying and prophesying exercised by freedwomen like Chloe.[23] The Spirit distributes gifts to Corinthian believers as members of the one body (they must reconsider and dismantle the party divisions, i.e., I belong to Paul, I belong to Apollos, I belong to Chloe). Yet they can (mis)use those gifts without love. Paul is not seeking to create a panacea or a universally applicable definition of love. Nor is it prescriptive for everyone, but it targets those who are part of the problem and whom Paul wishes to subordinate, which includes Apollos and women who pray and prophesy with uncovered heads. The incorrect or loveless exercise of spiritual gifts is a source of strife and disorder.

Apparently, according to Paul's argument, although the Spirit gives the gifts, that alone does not guarantee that people will lovingly exercise them, in the way Paul prescribes—at least not in

22. Bazzana (*Having the Spirit of Christ*, 194) examines "glossolalia" in the context of Paul's patriarchal understanding of gender relations in 1 Corinthians.

23. Wire, *The Corinthian Women Prophets*.

Corinth (13:1–3)! The love that Paul describes and prescribes as a mechanism against the abuse and ineffective use of spiritual gifts is overwhelmingly passive (13:4–7). The Corinthians should rejoice in all that Paul has defined as true spiritual knowledge as opposed to worldly knowledge (see chapter 3). Paul's truth is not a champion of freedom but of the status quo: "Remain as you are when God called you" (1 Cor 7:20).

Howard Thurman's grandmother, Nancy Ambrose, rejected most of the Pauline corpus because of admonitions that the enslaved submit to their enslavers as an act of loyalty to God or Christ. Yet Ambrose found chapter 13 of 1 Corinthians useful, extracting it from its literary and historical context where Paul promotes a gendered hierarchy that subordinates women to men and a normalized gender binary. Marcia Riggs challenges Black men and women to be aware of the ways that we are complicit in sexual-gender oppression in the Black church (and beyond). Riggs warns that,

> apparently caught in reactive postures stemming from the psychological adaptation of dominant culturally based sexual-gender social myths [i.e., Black men as powerless, weak, and undependable; Black women as strong, physically invincible, and emotionally unfeeling], African American women and men tend to fulfill unspoken, coercive expectations [i.e., good Black women support Black men, defend Black culture, and so on, regardless; good Black men protect Black women, enact the role of fatherhood, provide for the family, define Black culture] in their sexual-gender relations. Both women and men thus act daily in complicity with sexual-gender oppression.[24]

Women are routinely encouraged and expected to silently bear and endure all things in their personal and social relationships in both private and public spaces. Love cannot exist without open and honest dialogue among equals. Real dialogue cannot exist in a context of gender subordination and silencing. Paulo Freire states the following about love:

24. Riggs, *Plenty Good Room*, 53.

> Love is at the same time the foundation of dialogue and dialogue itself. It is thus necessarily the task of responsible Subjects and cannot exist in a relation of domination. Domination reveals the pathology of love: sadism in the dominator [oppressor] and masochism in the dominated [oppressed]. Because love is an act of courage, not of fear, love is commitment to others. No matter where the oppressed are found, the act of love is commitment to their cause, to the cause of liberation. And this commitment, because it is loving, is dialogical. As an act of bravery, love cannot be sentimental; as an act of freedom, it must not serve as a pretext for manipulation. It must generate other acts of freedom; otherwise, it is not love.[25]

Shawn Copeland argues that virtues like patience, long-suffering, forbearance, love, faith, and hope must be reevaluated in the context of Black women's experiences.[26] The Pauline theology that asserts that love never fails without regard for historical context, systemic and structural barriers, violence, and generational trauma is often used to promote silence and forbearance as the ultimate godly response to intimate partner violence, racism, sexism, classism, and other oppressions resident in church, home, and society. But our liberation demands a creative response rather than a reactive ones. Riggs argues that reactive responses hold us captive to and maintain "white racist-sexist-capitalist oppression as well as perpetuate sexual-gender oppression within the African American community."[27] Stewart posits that "uninterrogated normative ideologies of patriarchal marriage [in sacred texts and contexts, including Pauline texts] . . . penetrated the heart of Black marital arrangements and expectations for a century and a half. . . . [Given Black people's struggle for love in this country, one must ask] whether patriarchal marriage is what the Black community really needs."[28] Paul is certainly advocating for patriarchal household structures and relationships among the believers in which men are

---

25. Freire, *Pedagogy of the Oppressed*, 70–71.

26. Copeland, "Wading through Many Sorrows," 151.

27. Riggs, *Plenty Good Room*, 54.

28. Stewart, *Black Women, Black Love*, 93.

the head, rather than for equal partnerships and unmitigated freedom. Clarice Martin questions Black people's willingness to critique
and reject enslavement in the household codes but their inability to
interrogate the mandate that a woman submit to a man as head of
the household in those same codes.[29] Addressing the violent impact
of patriarchalism on Black men, Black women, and Black families,
Stewart writes the following:

> Over time, America's violent structural exclusion of
> Black men from patriarchy has served unfortunately
> and unfairly to illuminate their widely perceived in-
> adequacies as men, husbands, and fathers. In this way,
> patriarchy and patriarchal marriage injure heterosexual
> Black men (and queer Black men to be sure), the women
> [or men] they love, and the children they bring into the
> world. Yet patriarchy also strips Black women of their in-
> dependence, authority, and decision-making power over
> their labor, their lives, and their love.[30]

Black women are expected to love and give sacrificially, at the
cost of self-love and wholeness. Their own well-being, dignity, hap-
piness, and vocation are forfeited for the sake of Black manhood,
toxic masculinity, children, family, church, and other institutions
while they are simultaneously subjugated. The dominant society
with the help of social scientific research has attempted to per-
suade people of color to view their relationships through the lens
of white patriarchal heteronormativity, which is often undergirded
by a theology of failed love. Black women and women of color are
accused of failing to love their men and communities if they do
not imitate white patriarchal love demonstrated in submission to
male headship theo-ideology. bell hooks states the following about
patriarchy and love:

> Patriarchy has always seen love as women's work as de-
> graded and devalued labor. And it has not cared when
> women failed to learn how to love, for patriarchal men
> have been the most willing to substitute care for love,

29. Martin, "Haustafeln."

30. Stewart, *Black Women, Black Love,* 97.

submission for respect. We did not need a feminist movement to let us know that females are more likely to be concerned with relationships, connections, and community than are males. Patriarchy trains us for this role. We do need a feminist [or womanist] movement to remind us again and again that love cannot exist in a context of domination, that the love we seek cannot be found as long as we are bound and not free.[31]

What does 1 Corinthians 13 have to say to Black women, queer identified people, and other women who live daily with the trauma of misogyny, racism, classism, dis-abilism, heterosexism, and the intersectionality of oppressions and violence? How do Black women and men love themselves and others while rejecting their subordination and oppressions? A female child victimized by sexual abuse and neglect would find it confusing, at the very least, if asked to embrace a love that is unconditionally long-suffering; that requires her to endure all things, to esteem others better than herself, including her abusers. Such a love would require a denial of her own experiences, abuse, and oppression. Women and children who have experienced abuse generally need time and space to recover a sense of self-worth and identity before they are able to risk loving others in wholesome ways.

Most victims of sexual abuse are women, and most often they are victimized by men, men whom they know. Unbridled patriarchy takes and is never satiated, especially when men themselves struggle for wholeness due to the trauma of classism, racism, heterosexism, and other forms of oppression that diminish one's sense of self and self-love. When that self is constructed as "manhood" predicated on the panacea of female submissiveness, women's sense of self-embodied wholeness must be sacrificed to the patriarchal gods who insist that women's love endure all things.

31. hooks, *Communion: The Female Search for Love*, xvi–xvii.

THE GIFTED BODY, LOVELESS GIFTS, AND EMBODIED LOVE

When we critically read Paul's "love chapter" in the context of the gendered hierarchies of knowledge and bodies, we must rethink the notion that Paul's characterization of love is a universal remedy for successful relationships. Paul did not intend it so. And if he did, it would still be problematic. First Corinthians 13 is part of the rhetorical strategy woven through the rest of the letter that promotes a gender hierarchy that privileges dominant heterosexual elite men while encouraging the submission of enslaved, freed, and lower-class freeborn women and men.

The only way that one can acknowledge Jesus as "Lord" or refrain from cursing Jesus's name (12:3) is by God's Spirit. From the Spirit originates, discriminately, a variety of gifts, services, activities that are provided for the common good of all (12:7, 11). The gifts Paul lists to make his point are wisdom, knowledge, faith, healing, working of miracles, prophecy, discernment of spirits, tongues/languages, interpretation of languages (12:8–10). Everyone belongs to one body; in Christ all members are baptized into the body of Christ. This specifically includes "Jews or Greeks, the enslaved or the freeborn" (12:13). However, the phrase "women and men" does not here constitute a social category that is transcended or overcome by inclusion in the body. Paul strategically omitted the phrase "men and women" despite its inclusion in the pre-Pauline baptismal formula that we find in his Letter to the Galatians (3:28): "there is neither male nor female, enslaved nor freeborn, Jew nor gentile." Both formulas maintain and normalize binaries. What about the freedwoman or man? Thus, at 12:13 Paul argues for a unity that erases some (and ignores others) ethnic (Jew and gentile) and social (slave and free) hierarchies, at least concerning spiritual gifts, but not those based on gender. Jouette Bassler argues that Paul most likely omitted the gender binary "because including it would undermine his already torturous argument in Chapter 11 concerning the wearing of status-marking veils."[32] If Paul had included the erasure of gender hierarchy in his baptismal formula in 1

32. Bassler, "1 Corinthians," 564.

Corinthians, he would have undermined rhetorical arguments constructed throughout the letter that subordinate men to women.

Paul says each and every body part belongs to the whole body and is necessary for the functioning of the body; an interdependency exists among the parts, just as it does among men and women in 1 Corinthians 7 and 11:2–16. Paul implicitly argues that some are weaker, *less* honorable, and *less* respectable than others, and some are even inferior to others (12:22–25). The weaker are indispensable, the less honorable are clothed with more honor and the less respectable are treated with more respect. In order to combat dissension or division God has given more honor to the inferior members. Perhaps, Paul has in mind that the women are the weaker, less honorable, less respectable members of the body. But the honor that women exhibit (or the shame they avoid) is in the covering of their hair while praying and prophesying, which is also a symbol of their subordinate (inferior, weaker) status in relation to men as the head. The body respects women's gifts; rejoices in their honor, despite their inferior status (12:26).

The image of body parts, despite the rhetoric of interdependence, does not encourage a vision of wholeness for the individual who suffers from a fragmented life caused by oppression and violence. To visualize oneself as a weak, less honorable, and inferior part of a body or community, as opposed to fully embodied is to see oneself in a fragmented way connected to others in terms of one's own weakness and the other's strength; one's own lack of honor and another's honor; one's own lack of respect and the respectability of others. This is the way in which Black women and men, people of color and poor people have been encouraged to see themselves in relation to their oppressors and the dominant patriarchal society. Black people, people of color, Black women more specifically, have been taught implicitly and explicitly to be conscious of or to hate their body parts. Emilie Townes asserts that "to love the mouth, the eyes, the hands, the neck, the heart—to love the body is radical ontology within structured domination and control. The concerns for concrete material well-being *and* spiritual wholeness are imperatives in the post-modern context for African Americans."[33] Gilkes avers that "where our bodies and our appearance are concerned, because of the many mixed messages from within and outside of African-American culture, we are loved and troubled almost constantly."[34]

Paul does not emphasize love among members of the body or the practice of self-love for each member, but, as already noted, his focus is love in relation to the function of spiritual gifts for the benefit of the body. What happens when the needs of individual members do not coincide with or conflict with the needs of the body? What happens when meeting the needs of the corporate body of believers to the exclusion of certain members is oppressive and abusive to those members?

The problem with Paul's list of spiritual gifts is that it gives the impression of being an exhaustive list. In fact, God's gift of self-control(?) that Paul claims for himself at 1 Corinthians 7:7 is not listed among the spiritual gifts in chapter 12. Black women's contextual experience of active resistance or dissent from oppressive patriarchalism is a gift of the Spirit empowered by a love of self and community. Civil and voting rights activist Fannie Lou Hamer said that her Christian mother taught her to practice active resistance but never without love.

In 1 Corinthians 13, kindness and long-suffering are manifestations of love. But it is important that we ask in what context are kindness and long-suffering the enemy of self-love? Copeland writes that in "their resistance, Black women's suffering redefined caricatured Christian virtues. Because of the lives and suffering of Black women held in chattel slavery, the meanings of forbearance, long-suffering, patience, love, hope, and faith can never again be ideologized."[35]

Black women in America have always had to struggle for love, through love, and in love. As enslaved Africans and as African

33. Townes, "To Be Called Beloved," 190. In this essay, Townes explores lynching in the eighteenth and nineteenth centuries and racism in both north and south; the dumping of toxic waste in poor Black communities, poverty, and the impact of Black neoconservatism.

34. Gilkes, "The 'Loves' and 'Troubles' of African-American Women's Bodies," 84.

35. Copeland, "'Wading through Many Sorrows,'" 153–54.

Americans negotiating life in freedom, they have been coerced and forced into loveless, illicit sexual relationships with white enslavers/masters; coerced and forced to breed with enslaved Black men to increase the property holdings of their enslavers. Black women have been prohibited from marrying the Black men (and nonBlack men and women) they have loved, encouraged to stay in relationships where love went south or sour, told that they as a racial gender group are unlikely to marry or find love, accused of being emasculators of Black men and the cause of decline in the Black nuclear family. Black women, and women generally, have been encouraged by religious folks to stay in loveless, violent marriages for the sake of children and Black men's gifts, well-being, reputations, and souls.

According to Paul, a man or woman can be gifted and loveless. Just as one can be married, unmarried, or in a committed monogamous relationship without love. Love is decontextualized and universalized with no regard for diversity of bodies, human experience, or cultural context. Regardless of context, readers are encouraged to bear, believe, hope, and endure "all things" in demonstration of a love that will not fail (13:7–8), which implies that what is most important is longevity (i.e., how long one remains in a relationship, even if it is an abusive relationship). Longevity becomes equated with quality or the measure of quality.

Human love is *embodied* love. Embodiment cannot escape the particularity of the individual or collective body, its situatedness. Townsend Gilkes argues that "all human experience is embodied experience and the consequences of cultural humiliation are most dramatically shown in reference to the body. Not only is experience embodied, but stereotypes, pernicious cultural representations of people, are also embodied images. All racial stereotypes are usually named images attached to an image of a body, and all of those named images are gendered."[36]

---

36. Gilkes, "The 'Loves' and 'Troubles' of African-American Women's Bodies," 92–93.

CHOOSING HOPE AND SELF-LOVE

Howard Thurman asserted that "love is possible only between two freed spirits."[37] Perhaps this is why enslaved Africans privileged hope (for freedom) over love. Clenora Hudson-Weems argues that Black women and men must recover what we have lost or traded for a love-less, self-less Pauline sexual ethics grounded in oppressive patriarchal love:

> If all Africana men respected the original reality of the equality of both sexes in African cosmology, then they would refuse to continue to allow external forces, such as nontraditional African religions and alien political family structures wherein female subjugation is inherent, to influence their lives and ways. The end result would be that Africana people (men and women) the world over would then collectively struggle toward recovering their natural birthright as determiners of their fate as a liberated people, dedicated to their families and their future generations.[38]

African American pastor ordained in AME Zion Church Frances Spearing Randolph (1866–1951) preached a sermon from 1 Corinthians 13:13 entitled "Hope." She proclaimed that "when all else has gone out of life, hope is still left." Randolph argued that human beings "would die but not hope sustain" them for when all else fails, hope remains. What the "Negro race" needs, according to Randolph, in the twentieth century, facing the problem of the color line, is *hope*, which engenders perseverance; success, she argued "is gained only by perseverance."[39] Hope chooses perseverance, wills survival, and insists on self-love. Gilkes states, "If, through loving ourselves 'regardless' and repairing our inner visions, we save our own lives, we have taken the first step toward our 'response-ability' to save our brothers and sisters. Self-love then is probably the most critical task we complete in establishing our commitment 'to survival and wholeness of entire people,' male and female."[40] When

---

37. Thurman, *Jesus and the Disinherited*, 101.

38. Hudson-Weems, *Africana Womanism*, 144.

39. Randolph, "Hope."

40. Gilkes, "The 'Loves' and 'Troubles' of African-American Women's Bodies," 97.

one tries to practice other-centered love without self-love, that other-centered love will demand we sacrifice or destroy the self-love to which the Divine calls us, and sooner or later the self and the other will become a source and object of contempt and hate.

Townes asserts that "at the heart of a womanist ontology is the self-other relation grounded in concrete existence and succored in the flawed transcendent powers of our spirituality."[41] We must guard against both a selfish individualism and a disavowal of the significant contextual embodied self. Townes further writes that "to remember our fleshiness is to recognize that dualistic oppositions such as self-other, egoism-altruism, theory-practice, individual-community, and mind-body are interactive and interdependent in an ontology of wholeness."[42] Each informs the other and impacts the other, in positive and negative ways. "We are, in the most basic sense, each other's keeper."[43] It is equally important that we continue to make her-stories of resistance and rebellion as expressions of embodied self-love. The wholeness Black men and women strive for is based in contextual community values such as hope.[44]

A womanist approach to life emphasizes and affirms the necessity of re-membering or embodying the self-love and hope that a hostile world attempts to destroy through racism, classism, neocolonialism, sexism, misogynoir, and heterosexism or homophobia. Gilkes posits this about the importance of Black women's self-love in a hostile world:

> Cultural humiliation assaults Black women by undermining their capacities for self-love. A womanist approach to life and living underscores the importance of self-love for celebrating and resisting in a hostile society. . . . The ethical challenge to live out the mandates of love in a hateful and hate-filled world is a constant struggle and demands an attitude of resistance that must be

41. Townes, "To Be Called Beloved," 200.

42. Townes, "To Be Called Beloved," 201.

43. Townes, "To Be Called Beloved," 201.

44. Townes, "To Be Called Beloved," 201.

embraced through what bell hooks calls "a process of critical remembering."[45]

Re-membering who we are and were created to be is a strategy of hope. "Hope is a discipline," is what a nun told the abolitionist Mariame Kaba; it is not optimism.[46] As a discipline, Kaba asserts, hope is something "we have to [choose and] practice every single day. Because in the world we live in, it's easy to feel a sense of hopelessness, . . . that nothing is going to change ever."[47] We embody this hope until we free us! We discipline ourselves to re-member what the challenges of life can make us forget. We re-member that our labor is not in vain. We re-member that self-love and the love of others requires risk! We are capable; we are loved; and we are loving and lovable. We do not have to settle for a patriarchal love that devours us. We deserve and are worthy of unmitigated freedom. We hope for what is not yet seen, the yet to be, the can be, and will be, a different life-giving embodied love that insists on parity and partnership; that respects our bodies, voices, choices, dreams, desires (sexual and nonsexual), gifts, and achievements. Now three—faith, hope, and love—barely survive, but what we now need most is hope. We choose the discipline of hope.

45. Gilkes, "The 'Loves' and 'Troubles' of African-American Women's Bodies," 82.

46. Kaba, *We Do This 'Til We Free Us*, 26.

47. Kaba, *We Do This 'Til We Free Us*, 27.

CHAPTER 6

Epilogue

What Has Paul to Do with Us Now?

Chloe and Her People is the first book-length womanist reading of 1 Corinthians, and I hope it is not the last one. There is always more to know, to know differently, that needs to be said and said differently, which speaks to every reading as epistemologically contested space. In this book, I attempted to resurrect the voices of formerly enslaved women, freedwomen, slumbered in sacred artifacts, ancient and modern, and sharing a name, naming a traumatic past and the experience of life in stigmatized bodies. This space is necessary, space for dialogue, long overdue, that centers Black women who embody, produce, and disseminate wholistic knowledge that is simultaneously, organically, and mutually divine and human, so that we might interrogate the schizophrenic splitting of ourselves in two between the God who reveals God's self to us and the will of Paul. This book is a witness of the unapologetic prioritization of Black women and men's struggle for love in enslavement and in freedom, a refusal to settle for love-less couplings and self-less love sold by enslavers or an apostle. Black people are not new to impending crises. Black women and men perennially strive for and negotiate love within the crises of racism, sexism, queerphobia, poverty, classism, bibliolatry, and under the gaze of the dominant. Monogamy has generally been love's hope, but we stumbled into the trap of love-patriarchy and patriarchal marriage. This book, *Chloe and Her People*, is dissent. It is womanist talk and sass and throwing shade at Paul's lust-focused sexual ethics, at his gendered head logic, and at his passive self-less love.

What Has Paul to Do with Us Now? Paul and Us, we will continue our dialogue. No, I don't hate him; it is not personal. Or maybe it is, personal and political, for Paul and for me. But this dialogue, this talk back is necessary. Just as Luke's Jesus returned again and again to eat and dispute with some Pharisees, I will return to the rhetorical table Paul has set and the meal he has prepared. But I insist upon a potluck, so that I too can contribute to the feast and am not mistaken for the meal. We have much to chew on, like resurrection of the body, kingdom language, the lists of vices, the Lord's supper, bringing lawsuits against members of the community, and more on enslavement. It might become heated, but I will return to your table and invite you to mine.

Bibliography

Adams, Susan. "White High School Drop-Outs Are as Likely to Land Jobs as Black College Students." Forbes.com, June 27, 2014.

Ahmed, Afia. "The Clothes of My Faith." In *It's Not about the Burqa: Muslim Women on Faith, Feminism, Sexuality and Race*, edited by Mariam Khan, 65–77. London: Picador, 2019.

Amjad-Ali, Christine. "The Equality of Women: Form or Substance (1 Corinthians 11:2–16)." In *Voices from the Margin: Interpreting the Bible in the Third World*, edited by R. S. Sugirtharajah, 185–93. Maryknoll, NY: Orbis, 1995.

Archer, R. L. "Apollos and the Logos Doctrine." *Expository Times* 62.10 (1951) 301–3.

Ashcroft, Bill, Gareth Griffiths, and Hellen Tiffin. *Postcolonial Studies: The Key Concepts*. 3rd ed. London: Routledge, 2013.

Avalos, Hector. "Circumcision as a Slave Mark." *Perspectives in Religious Studies* 43.3 (2015) 259–74.

Bacon, Thomas, and William Meade. *Sermons Addressed to Masters and Servants and Published in the Year 1943*. Winchester, UK: Heiskell, 1943. HeinOnline.

Baldwin, James. *The Fire Next Time*. New York: Vintage, 1992.

Barrett, C. K. *A Commentary on the First Epistle to the Corinthians*. London: Adam and Charles Bloch, 1968.

Barton, George A. "Some Influences of Apollos in the New Testament." *Journal of Biblical Literature* 43.1–2 (1924) 207–23.

Bassler, Jouette. "1 Corinthians." In *Women's Commentary of the Bible*, edited by Carol A. Newsom, Sharon H. Ringe, and Jacqueline E. Lapsley, 557–65. Louisville: Westminster John Knox, 2012.

Bazzana, Giovanni B. *Having the Spirit of Christ: Spirit Possession and Exorcism in the Early Christian Groups*. New Haven, CT: Yale University Press, 2020.

Bell, Sinclair, and Teresa Ramsby. Introduction to *Free at Last! The Impact of Freed Slaves on the Empire*, edited by Sinclair Bell and Teresa Ramsby, 1–24. London: Bloomsbury, 2013.

Bonilla-Silva, Eduardo, and David Dietrich. "The Sweet Enchantment of Color-Blind Racism in Obamerica." *Annals of the American Academy of Political and Social Science* 634 (2011) 190–206.

Bowens, Lisa M. *African American Readings of Paul: Reception, Resistance and Transformation*. Grand Rapids: Eerdmans, 2020.

Bradley, Keith. *Slavery and Society at Rome*. Cambridge: Cambridge University Press, 1994.

Braxton, Brad. *No Longer Slaves: Galatians and African American Experience*. Collegeville, MN: Liturgical, 2002.

Briggs, Sheila. "Paul on Bondage and Freedom in Imperial Roman Society." In *Paul and Politics: Ekklesia, Israel, Imperium, Interpretation*, edited by Richard Horsley, 110–23. Harrisburg, PA: Trinity, 2000.

Brooten, Bernadette J. "Enslaved Women in Basil of Caesarea's Canonical Letters: An Intersectional Analysis." In *Doing Gender—Doing Religion: Fallstudien zur Intersektionalität im frühen Judentum, Christentum und Islam*, edited by Ute E. Eisen et al., 325–55. Tübingen: Mohr Siebeck, 2013.

Brown, Michael Joseph. "An Inconsistent Truth: The New Testament, Early Christianity, and Sexuality." In *The Sexual Politics of Black Churches*, edited by Josef Sorett, 50–64. New York: Columbia University Press, 2022.

Byrd, Ayana D., and Lori L. Tharps. *Hair Story: Untangling the Roots of Black Hair in America*. Rev. ed. New York: St. Martin's, 2014.

Cardona, Crhistian. "Paul Epistemology: A Sketch of Divine Knowledge in 1 Corinthians 1:18—2:16." *Perspectives in Religious Studies* 49.3 (2022) 271–86.

Castelli, Elizabeth. *Imitating Paul: A Discourse of Power*. Louisville: Westminster John Knox, 1991.

Charles, Ronald L. *Paul and the Politics of Diaspora*. Minneapolis: Fortress, 2014.

Chow, John K. "Patronage in Roman Corinth." In *Paul and Empire: Religion and Power in Roman Imperial Society*, edited by Richard A. Horsley, 104–25. Minneapolis: Fortress, 1997.

Civil Rights History Project. Rosie Head oral history interview conducted by John Dittmer in Tchula, Mississippi. March 13, 2013. Library of Congress. https://www.loc.gov/item/2015669173/.

Concannon, Cavan W. *Profaning Paul*. Chicago: University of Chicago Press, 2021.

Copeland, M. Shawn. "Wading through Many Sorrows: Toward a Theology of Suffering in a Womanist Perspective." In *Womanist Theological Ethics: A Reader*, edited by Katie Geneva Cannon et al., 135–54. Louisville: Westminster John Knox, 2011.

Craft, William, and Ellen Craft. *Running a Thousand Miles for Freedom; or, The Escape of William and Ellen Craft from Slavery*. In *Slave Narratives*, edited by William L. Andrews and Henry Louis Gates Jr., 677–742. Lanham, MD: Library of America, 2000.

Davis, Viola. "Interview on Wearing Her Natural Hair." YouTube video, 5:18, posted September 24, 2013. https://youtu.be/jUDGmmZaidU.

De Groot, Kristen. "Iran Protests, Explained." PennToday.org, September 29, 2022. https://penntoday.upenn.edu/news/iran-protests-explained.

Den Dulk, Matthijs. "Aquila and Apollos: Acts 18 in Light of Ancient Ethnic Stereotypes." *Journal of Biblical Literature* 139.1 (2020) 177–89.

Douglass, Frederick. *Narrative of the Life of Frederick Douglass, an American Slave. Written by Himself (1845)*. In *Slave Narratives*, edited by William L. Andrews and Henry Louis Gates, 267–368. Lanham, MD: Library of America, 2000.

Drewel, Henry John. "Crowning Glories: Hair, Head, Style, and Substance in Yoruba Culture." In *Tenderheaded: A Comb-Bending Collection of Hair Stories*, edited by Juliette Harris and Pamela Johnson, 227–36. New York: Washington Square, 2001.

Edwards, Breanna. "Court: School District Dress Code Discriminated against Students with Locs." Essence.org, November 4, 2020. https://www.essence.com/news/deandre-arnold-kaden-bradford-locs-discrimination/.

Eugenios, Jillian. "Gabby Douglas' Mom Weighs in on Hair Controversy." NBCNews.com, October 27, 2012. https://www.nbcnews.com/news/world/gabby-douglas-mom-weighs-hair-controversy-flna928488.

Far, Tara Sepehri. "Woman Dies in Custody of Iran's 'Morality Police.'" HumanRightsWatch.org, September 16, 2022. https://www.hrw.org/news/2022/09/16/woman-dies-custody-irans-morality-police.

Felder, Cain Hope. *Troubling Biblical Waters: Race, Class and Family*. Maryknoll, NY: Orbis, 1990.

Fiorenza, Elisabeth Schüssler. *Rhetoric and Ethic: The Politics of Biblical Studies*. Minneapolis: Fortress, 1999.

———. "Slave Wo/Men and Freedom: Some Methodological Reflections." In *Postcolonial Interventions: Essays in Honor of R. S. Sugirtharajah*, edited by Tat-siong Benny Liew, 123–46. Sheffield, UK: Sheffield Phoenix, 2009.

———. "Paul and the Politics of Interpretation." In *Paul and Politics: Ekklesia, Israel, Imperium, Interpretation. Essays in Honor of Krister Stendahl*, edited by Richard A. Horsley, 40–57. Harrisburg, PA: Trinity, 2000.

Fitzgerald, William. "The Slave, between Absence and Presence." In *Unspoken Rome: Absence in Latin Literature and Its Reception*, edited by Tom Geue and Elena Giusti, 239–49. New York: Cambridge University Press, 2021.

Fitzmyer, Joseph A. "*Kephale* in 1 Corinthians 11:3." *Interpretation* 47 (1995) 52–59.

Franklin, James L., Jr. "Pantomimists at Pompeii: Actius Anicetus and His Troupe." *American Journal of Philology* 108.1 (1987) 95–107.

Fredriksen, Paula. *Paul: The Pagans' Apostle*. New Haven, CT: Yale University Press, 2017.

Freire, Paulo. *Pedagogy of the Oppressed*. New York: Continuum, 1997.

Gardner, Eric. "*The Complete Fortune Teller and Dream Book*: An Antebellum Text 'by Chloe Russel, a Woman of Colour.'" *New England Quarterly* 78.2 (2005) 259–88.

Gilkes, Cheryl Townsend. "The 'Loves' and 'Troubles' of African-American Women's Bodies. The Womanist Challenge to Cultural Humiliation and Community Ambivalence." In *Womanist Theological Ethics: A Reader*, edited by Katie Geneva Cannon et al., 81–97. Louisville: Westminster John Knox, 2011.

Given, Mark. *Paul's True Rhetoric: Ambiguity, Cunning, and Deception in Greece and Rome*. Harrisburg, PA: Trinity, 2001.

Glancy, Jennifer A. *Slavery in Early Christianity*. Minneapolis: Fortress, 2006.

Guy, Lindsey. "Wasting Time at the End of the World: Queer Failure, Unproductivity, and Unintelligibility in 1 Corinthians." In *Bodies on the Verge: Queering Pauline Epistles*, edited by Joseph Marchal, 63–82. Atlanta: Society of Biblical Literature, 2019.

Hamilton, Alesha. "Untangling Discrimination: The Crown Act and Protecting Black Hair" *University of Cincinnati Law Review* 89.2 (2020) 483–508.

Harper, Frances E. Watkins. *Sketches of Southern Life*. Philadelphia: Ferguson, 1891.

Harrill, Albert J. "Revisiting the Problem of 1 Corinthians 7:21." *Biblical Research* 65 (2020) 77–94.

Hartman, Midori. "A Little *Porneia* Leavens the Whole: Queer(ing) Limits of Community in 1 Corinthians 5." In *Bodies on the Verge: Queering Pauline Epistles*, edited by Joseph A. Marchal, 143–63. Atlanta: Society of Biblical Literature, 2019.

Hezser, Catherine. *Jewish Slavery in Antiquity*. New York: Oxford University Press, 2005.

Hill, Patricia Liggins. "'Let Me Make the Songs for the People': A Study of Frances Watkins Harper's Poetry." *Black American Literature Forum* 15.2 (1981) 60–65.

hooks, bell. *Communion: The Female Search for Love*. New York: Perennial, 2002.

Horsley, Richard A. "1 Corinthians: A Case Study of Paul's Assembly as an Alternative Society." In *Paul and Empire: Religion and Power in Roman Imperial Society*, edited by Richard A. Horsley, 241–52. Minneapolis: Fortress, 1997.

Hudson-Weems, Clenora. *Africana Womanism: Reclaiming Ourselves*. Troy, MI: Bedford, 1995.

Jackson, Janet. *Janet Jackson*. A Lifetime television documentary miniseries, 2022.

Jaima, Amir R. A. "American Ignorance and the Discourse of Manageability Concerning the Care and Presentation of Black Hair." *Journal of Medical Humanities* 43.2 (2022) 283–302.

Jodamus, Johnathan. "Gender Ideology and Power in 1 Corinthians." *Journal of Early Christian History* 6.1 (2016) 29–58.

Johnson, E. Patrick. "'Quare' Studies, or (Almost) Everything I Know about Queer Studies I Learned from My Grandmother." In *Black Queer Studies: A Critical Anthology*, edited by E. Patrick Johnson and Mae G. Henderson, 124–57. Durham, NC: Duke University Press, 2005.

Johnson, Oliver. *William Lloyd Garrison and His Times; or, Sketches of the Anti-Slavery Movement in America, and of the Man Who Was Its Founder and Moral Leader*. Boston: Houghton, Miffline, 1879. HeinOnline.

Johnson-DeBaufre, Melanie, and Laura S. Nasrallah. "Beyond the Heroic Paul: Toward a Feminist and Decolonizing Approach to the Letters of Paul." In *The Colonized Apostle: Paul through Postcolonial Eyes*, edited by Christopher Stanley, 161–74. Minneapolis: Fortress, 2011.

Jory, E. J. "Associations of Actors in Rome." *Hermes* 98.2 (1970) 224–53.

Joshel, Sandra R., and Lauren Hackworth Petersen. *The Material Life of Roman Slaves*. Cambridge: Cambridge University Press, 2017.

Kaba, Mariame. *We Do This 'Til We Free Us: Abolitionist Organizing and Transforming Justice*. Chicago: Haymarket, 2021.

———. "When Black Hair Tangles with White Power." In *Tenderheaded: A Comb-Bending Collection of Hair Stories*, edited by Juliette Harris and Pamela Johnson, 102–8. New York: Washington Square, 2001.

Ker, Donald P. "Paul and Apollos—Colleagues or Rivals?" *Journal for the Study of the New Testament* 77 (2000) 75–97.

Kim, Yung Suk. *Christ's Body in Corinth: The Politics of a Metaphor*. Minneapolis: Fortress, 2008.

Kleijwegt, Marc. "Deciphering Freedwomen in the Roman Empire." In *Free at Last! The Impact of Freed Slaves on the Empire*, edited by Sinclair Bell and Teresa Ramsby, 110–29. London: Bloomsbury, 2013.

Knox, J. *Chapters in a Life of Paul*. London: SCM, 1989.

Kremer, Gary R. *George Washington Carver: In His Own Words*. 2nd ed. Columbia: University of Missouri, 2017.

Labinjoh, Justin. "The Sexual Life of the Oppressed: An Examination of the Family Life of Ante-Bellum Slaves." *Phylon* 35.4 (1974) 375–97.

Lavrinovica, Alesja. "The Syntactic Flexibility of 1 Corinthians 14:33b." *Journal of Biblical Literature* 141.1 (2022) 157–75.

Lieu, Judith. *Neither Jew nor Greek? Constructing Early Christianity*. 2nd ed. London: Bloomsbury T. & T. Clark, 2016.

Liew, Benny Tat-Siong. *Politics of Parousia: Reading Mark Inter(con)textually*. Boston: Brill, 1999.

———. "Redressing Bodies in Corinth: Racial/Ethnic Politics and Religious Difference in the Context of Empire." In *The Colonized Apostle: Paul through Postcolonial Eyes*, edited by Benny Liew, 75–97. Honolulu: University of Hawai'i Press, 2008.

Lintott, Andrew. "Freedmen and Slaves in the Light of Legal Documents from First-Century A.D. Campania." *Classical Quarterly* 52.2 (2002) 555–65.

Lo Bue, F. "The Historical Background of the Epistle to the Hebrews." *Journal of Biblical Literature* 75 (1956) 52–57.

Lorde, Audre. *Sister Outsider: Essays and Speeches.* Freedom, CA: Crossing, 1996.

Mabilishaka, Afiya M., et al. "Don't Get It Twisted: Untangling the Psychology of Hair Discrimination within Black Communities." *American Journal of Orthopsychiatry* 90.5 (2020) 590–99.

Marchal, Joseph, ed. *After the Corinthian Women Prophets: Reimagining Rhetoric and Power.* Atlanta: Society of Biblical Literature, 2021.

———. "Alternative Futures, Ephemeral Bodies: Untouching the Corinthian Women Prophets." In *After the Corinthian Women Prophets: Reimagining Rhetoric and Power,* edited by Joseph Marchal, 123–43. Atlanta: Society of Biblical Literature, 2021.

———, ed. *Bodies on the Verge: Queering Pauline Epistles.* Atlanta: Society of Biblical Literature, 2019.

———. *The Politics of Heaven: Women, Gender, and Empire in the Study of Paul.* Minneapolis: Fortress, 2008.

Marshall, Jill E. *Women Praying and Prophesying in Corinth.* Tübingen: Mohr Siebeck, 2017.

Martin, Clarice J. "The Eyes Have It: Slaves in the Communities of Christ-Believers." In *Christian Origins,* edited by Richard A. Horsley, 221–39. A People's History of Christianity 1. Minneapolis: Fortress, 2005.

———. "The Haustafeln (Household Codes) in African American Biblical Interpretation: 'Free Slaves' and 'Subordinate Women.'" In *Stony the Road We Trod: African American Biblical Interpretation,* edited by Cain Hope Felder, 206–31. Minneapolis: Fortress, 1991.

Martin, Dale B. *The Corinthian Body.* New Haven, CT: Yale University Press, 1995.

Martin, Patrick J. *Apollos: Paul's Partner or Rival?* Collegeville, MN: Liturgical, 2009.

Matthews, Shelly. "Hearing Wo/men Prophets: Intersections, Silences, Publics." In *After the Corinthian Women Prophets: Reimagining Rhetoric and* Power, edited by Joseph A. Marchal, 47–68. Atlanta: Society of Biblical Literature, 2021.

Mihaila, Corin. *The Paul-Apollos Relationship and Paul's Stance toward Greco-Roman Rhetoric.* London: T. & T. Clark, 2009.

Miller, Anna C. *Corinthian Democracy: Democratic Discourse in 1 Corinthians.* Eugene, OR: Pickwick, 2015.

———. "Not with Eloquent Wisdom: Democratic *Ekklēsia* Discourse in 1 Corinthians 1–4." *Journal for the Study of the New Testament* 35.4 (2013) 323–54.

———. "Out of House and Home: Early Christian Community as Public *Ekklesia.*" In *After the Corinthian Women Prophets: Reimagining Rhetoric and Power,* edited by Joseph A. Marchal, 165–94. Atlanta: Society of Biblical Literature, 2021.

Bibliography

Mitchell, Margaret M. *Paul and the Rhetoric of Reconciliation: An Exegetical Investigation of the Language and Composition of 1 Corinthians*. Louisville: Westminster John Knox, 1991.

Montefiore, H. W. *The Epistle to the Hebrews*. London: A&C Black, 1964.

Morrison, Toni. *The Source of Self-Regard*. New York: Vintage, 2019.

Moultrie, Monique. "Interrogating the Passionate and the Pious: Televangelism and Black Women's Sexuality." In *The Sexual Politics of Black Churches*, edited by Josef Sorett, 104–16. New York: Columbia University Press, 2022.

———. *Passionate and Pious: Religious Media and Black Women's Sexuality*. Durham, NC: Duke University Press, 2017.

Murphy-O'Connor, Jerome. "Sex and Logic in 1 Corinthians 11:2–16." *Conversations with the Biblical World* 42 (1980) 482–500.

Nasrallah, Laura Salah. "1 Corinthians." In *The New Testament Fortress Commentary on the Bible*, edited by Margaret Aymer, Cynthia Briggs Kittredge, and David A. Sánchez, 427–71. Minneapolis: Fortress, 2014.

———. *Archaeology and the Letters of Paul*. London: Oxford University Press, 2019.

———. "'You Were Bought with a Price': Freedpersons and Things in 1 Corinthians." In *Corinth in Contrast: Studies in Equality*, edited by Steven J. Friesen, Sarah A. James, and Daniel N. Schowalter, 54–73. Leiden: Brill, 2014.

Oldfather, W. A., trans. *Epictetus: The Discourses, Books III–IV*. Loeb Classical Library 218. Cambridge: Harvard University Press, 2000.

Osiek, Carolyn, and Margaret Y. MacDonald. *A Woman's Place: House Churches in Earliest Christianity*. With Janet H. Tulloch. Minneapolis: Fortress, 2006.

Oster, Richard E. "Use, Misuse and Neglect of Archaeological Evidence in Some Modern Works on 1 Corinthians (1 Cor 7,1–5; 8,10; 11,2–16; 12,14–26)." *Zeitschrift für die neutestamentliche Wissenschaft und die Kunde der älteren Kirche* 83.1–2 (1992) 52–73.

———. "When Men Wore Veils to Worship: The Historical Context of 1 Corinthians." *New Testament Studies* 11.4 (1988) 481–505.

Parker, Angela N. "Feminized-Minoritized Paul? A Womanist Reading of Paul's Body in the Corinthian Context." In *Minoritized Women Reading Race and Ethnicity, Minoritized Women Reading Race and Ethnicity*, edited by Mitzi J. Smith and Jin Young Choi, 71–88. Lanham, MD: Rowman & Littlefield, 2021.

Peters, Janelle. "Reading 1 Corinthians 11:1–16 through Habits and Hijabs in the United States." In *1 and 2 Corinthians*, edited by Yung Suk Kim, 129–45. Minneapolis: Fortress, 2013.

Petersen, L. H. *The Freedman in Roman Art and Art History*. Cambridge: Cambridge University Press, 2006.

Phillips, Layli. *The Womanist Reader*. London: Routledge, 2006.

Pickett, Ray. "Conflicts in Corinth." In *Christian Origins*, edited by Richard A. Horsley, 113–37. A People's History of Christianity 1. Minneapolis: Fortress, 2005.

Pilgrim, David. "The Picaninny Caricature." Ferris State University. Jim Crow Museum. October 2000; edited 2021. https://www.ferris.edu/HTMLS/news/jimcrow/antiblack/picaninny/homepage.htm.

Powery, Emerson B., and Rodney S. Sadler Jr. *The Genesis of Liberation: Biblical Interpretation in the Antebellum Narratives of the Enslaved.* Louisville: Westminster John Knox, 2016.

Ramsby, Teresa. "'Reading' the Freed Slave in the *Cena Trimalchionis.*" In *Free at Last! The Impact of Freed Slaves on the Empire,* edited by Sinclair Bell and Teresa Ramsby, 66–87. London: Bloomsbury, 2013.

Randolph, Frances Sperry. "Hope." In *Daughters of Thunder: Black Women Preachers and Their Sermons, 1850–1979*, edited by Bettye Collier-Thomas, 119–20. San Francisco: Jossey-Bass, 1998.

Reaves, Jayme, David Tombs, and Rocio Figueroa, eds. *When Did We See You Naked? Sexual Violence and Crucifixion.* London: SCM, 2021.

Richards, Akilah S. "How Blackgirl Natural Hair Is Shamed from Infancy to Adulthood." Everydayfeminism.com. August 28, 2014. https://everydayfeminism.com/2014/08/how-natural-hair-is-shamed/.

Riggs, Marcia Y. *Plenty Good Room: Women versus Male Power in the Black Church.* Eugene, OR: Wipf and Stock, 2008.

Ripat, Pauline. "Locating the Grapevine in the Late Republic: Freedmen and Communication." In *Free at Last! The Impact of Freed Slaves on the Empire,* edited by Sinclair Bell and Teresa Ramsby, 50–65. London: Bloomsbury, 2013.

Robbins, Bruce. *The Servant's Hand.* Durham, NC: Duke University Press, 1993.

Robert, Nikia Smith. "'Not Meant to Survive': Black Mothers Leading beyond the Criminal Line." In *Walking through the Valley: Womanist Explorations in the Spirit of Katie Geneva Cannon*, edited by Emilie M. Townes, Stacey M. Floyd-Thomas, Alison P. Gise Johnson, and Angela D. Sims, 107–19. Louisville: Westminster John Knox, 2022.

Ronnick, Michele Valerie. "'Saintly Souls': White Teachers' Advocacy and Instruction of Greek and Latin to African American Freedmen." In *Free at Last! The Impact of Freed Slaves on the Empire*, edited by Sinclair Bell and Teresa Ramsby, 177–95. London: Bloomsbury, 2013.

Saleem, Amna. "Shame, Shame, It Knows Your Name." In *It's Not about the Burqa: Muslim Women on Faith, Feminism, Sexuality and Race*, edited by Mariam Khan, 145–52. Picador: London, 2019.

Sanders, Boykin. "1 Corinthians." In *True to Our Native Land: An African American Commentary of the New Testament*, edited by Brian K. Blount, 276–306. Minneapolis: Fortress, 2007.

Schneemelcher, Wilhelm. *The Acts of Paul.* In *New Testament Apocrypha*, vol. 2, *Writings Relating to the Apostles, Apocalypses and Related Subjects*, edited by Wilhelm Schneemelcher, 237–70. English translation edited by R. McL. Wilson. Louisville: Westminster John Knox, 1989.

Sechrest, Love L. "Identity and the Embodiment of Privilege in Corinth." In *1 and 2 Corinthians*, edited by Yung Suk Kim, 9–30. Texts @ Contexts. Minneapolis: Fortress, 2013.

Sirvent, Roberto, and Duncan B. Reyburn, eds. *Theologies of Failure.* Eugene, OR: Wipf and Stock, 2019.

Smit, Joop F. M. "'What Is Apollos? What Is Paul?': In Search for the Coherence of First Corinthians 1:10—4:21." *Novum Testamentum* 44.3 (2002) 231–51.

Smith, Barbara. *Home Girls: A Black Feminist Anthology.* New York: Kitchen Table: Women of Color, 1983.

Smith, Mitzi J. "Epistemologies, Pedagogies, and the Subordinated Other: Luke's Parallel Construction of the Ethiopian Eunuch and the Alexandrian Apollos (Acts 8:26–40; 18:24–28)." In *Womanist Sass and Talk Back: Social (In)Justice, Intersectionality, and Biblical Interpretation*, edited by Mitzi J. Smith, 46–69. Eugene, OR: Cascade, 2018.

———. "Hagar Still *Ain't* Free: Paul's Counterterror Rhetoric, Constructed Identity, Enslavement, and Galatians 3:28." In *Minoritized Women Reading Race and Ethnicity*, edited by Mitzi J. Smith and Jin Young Choi, 45–70. Lanham, MD: Rowman & Littlefield, 2021.

———. *The Literary Construction of the Other in the Acts of the Apostles: Charismatic Others, the Jews, and Women.* Eugene, OR: Pickwick, 2011.

———. "Roman Slavery in Antiquity." In *Holy Bible: The African American Jubilee Edition, Contemporary English Version*, front matter edited by Cain Hope Felder, 157–85. New York: American Bible Society, 1999.

———. "Slavery in the Early Church." In *True to Our Native Land: An African American Commentary of the New Testament*, edited by Brian K. Blount et al., 11–22. Minneapolis: Fortress, 2007.

———. "This Little Light of Mine": The Womanist Biblical Scholar as Prophetess, Iconoclast, and Activist." In *I Found God in Me: A Womanist Biblical Hermeneutics Reader*, edited by Mitzi J. Smith, 109–27. Eugene, OR: Cascade, 2015.

———. "US Colonial Missions to African Slaves: Catechizing Black Souls, Traumatizing Black Bodies." In *Teaching All Nations: Interrogating the Matthean Great Commission*, edited by Mitzi Smith and Lalitha Jayachitra, 57–87. Minneapolis: Fortress, 2014.

———. "Utility, Fraternity, and Reconciliation: Ancient Slavery as a Context for the Return of Onesimus." In *Onesimus Our Brother: Reading Religion, Race and Culture in Philemon*, edited by Matthew V. Johnson et al., 47–48. Minneapolis: Fortress, 2012.

Smith, Mitzi J., and Michael W. Newheart. *We Are All Witnesses: Disruptive and Creative Biblical Interpretation.* Eugene, OR: Cascade, 2023.

Snorton, C. Riley. *Black on Both Sides: A Racial History of Trans Identity.* Minneapolis: University of Minnesota, 2017.

South Carolina Historical Society. The Register of Christ Church Parish (Continued). *South Carolina Historical and Genealogical Magazine* 22.1 (1921) 12–18.

Spicq, C. "L'Épitre aux Hébreux, Apollos, Jean-Baptiste, Les Héllenistes et Qumran." *Revue de Qumran* 1.3 (1959) 365–90.

Stewart, Dianne M. *Black Women, Black Love. American's War on African American Marriage*. New York: Seal, 2020.

Stewart, Maria W. "Mrs. Stewart's Address Speech to Her Friends in the City of Boston." September 21, 1833. Iowa State University. Archives of Women's Political Communication. https://awpc.cattcenter.iastate.edu/2020/11/20/mrs-stewarts-farewell-address-to-her-friends-in-the-city-of-boston-sept-21-1833/.

Stoneking, Lee. "The Power of a Woman's Uncut Hair." Sermon preached at Ladies Advance Conference 2007, Stockton, California. YouTube video, 1:32:29, posted April 1, 2020. https://www.youtube.com/watch?v=eNHHoBj8izs.

Stubbs, Roman. "A Wrestler Was Forced to Cut His Dreadlocks before a Match. His Town Is Still Looking for Answers." WashingtonPost.com, April 17, 2019. https://www.washingtonpost.com/sports/2019/04/17/wrestler-was-forced-cut-his-dreadlocks-before-match-his-town-is-still-looking-answers/.

Summers, Juana. "The History of Iran's So-Called Morality Police. NPR.org, September 30, 2022. https://www.npr.org/2022/09/30/1126281355/the-history-of-irans-so-called-morality-police.

Tertullian. *Le Voile des Vierges (De Virginibus Velandis)*. Paris: Cerf, 1997.

Thompson, Robin G. "Diaspora Jewish Freedmen: Stephen's Deadly Opponents." *Bibliotheca Sacra* 173 (2016) 166–81.

Thurman, Howard. *Jesus and the Disinherited*. Boston: Beacon, 1976.

Townes, Emilie M. "To Be Called Beloved: Womanist Ontology and Postmodern Refraction." In *Womanist Theological Ethics. A Reader*, editors Katie G. Cannon, Emilie M. Townes, and Angela D. Sims, 183–202. Louisville: Westminster John Knox, 2011.

Treggiari, Susan. "Libertine Ladies." *Classical World* 64.6 (1971) 196–98.

Tricomi, Albert. "Dialect and Identity in Harriet Jacobs's Autobiography and Other Slave Narratives." *Callaloo* 29.2 (2006) 619–33.

Tupamahu, Ekaputra. *Contesting Languages: Heteroglossia and the Politics of Language in the Early Church*. New York: Oxford University Press, 2022.

Umar, Charity. "Your Hair Your Glory: What the Bible Says about Our Natural Hair." YouTube video, 8:35, posted April 16, 2020. https://www.youtube.com/watch?v=65LWIcm6JOc.

Verboven, Koenraad. "The Freedman Economy of Roman Italy." In *Free at Last! The Impact of Freed Slaves on the Empire*, edited by Sinclair Bell and Teresa Ramsby, 88–109. London: Bloomsbury, 2013.

Virk, Kameron. "Ruby Williams: No Child with Afro Hair Should Suffer Like Me." BBC.com, February 10, 2020. https://www.bbc.com/news/newsbeat-45521094.

Bibliography

Walker, Alice. *In Search of Our Mothers' Gardens: Womanist Prose*. San Diego: Harcourt Brace, 1983.

———. "Oppressed Hair Puts a Ceiling on the Brain." In *Tenderheaded: A Comb-Bending Collection of Hair Stories*, edited by Juliette Harris and Pamela Johnson, 283–87. New York: Washington Square, 2001.

Wanamaker, Charles A. "Rhetoric and Power: Ideology and 1 Corinthians 1–4." In *Paul and the Corinthians: Studies on a Community in Conflict. Essays in Honor of Margaret Thrall*, edited by Trevor J. Burke and J. Keith Elliott, 115–37. Novum Testamentum Supplementum 109 Leiden: Brill, 2003.

Weems, Renita J. "The Biblical Field's Loss Was Womanist Ethics' Gain: Katie Cannon and the Dilemma of the Womanist Intellectual." In *Walking through the Valley: Womanist Explorations in the Spirit of Katie Geneva Cannon*, edited by Emilie M. Townes, Stacey M. Floyd-Thomas, Alison P. Gise Johnson, and Angela D. Sims, 3–12. Louisville: Westminster John Knox, 2022.

———. *What Matters Most: Ten Lessons in Living Passionately from the Song of Solomon*. New York: Warner, 2004.

Welborn, L. L. "On the Discord in Corinth: 1 Corinthians 1–4 and Ancient Politics." *Journal of Biblical Literature* 106.1 (1987) 85–111.

Wilson, Andrew. "Apostle Apollos?" *Journal of the Evangelical Theological Society* 56.2 (2013) 325–35.

Wilson, Harry Langford. "Latin Inscriptions at the Johns Hopkins University." *American Journal of Philology* 31.1 (1910) 25–42.

Wilson, Joseph A. P. "Recasting Paul as a Chauvinist within the Western Text-Type Manuscript Tradition: Implications for the Authorship Debate on 1 Corinthians 14:34–35. *Religions* 13.5 (2022) 1–18.

Wilson, Julee. "Haters Attach Gabby Douglas' Hair Again and Twitter Promptly Claps Back." Essence.com, October 27, 2020. https://www.essence.com/news/gabby-douglas-hair-haters-twitter-claps-back/.

Wire, Antoinette Clark. "1 Corinthians." In *Searching the Scriptures*, vol. 2, *A Feminist Commentary*, edited by Elisabeth Schüssler Fiorenza, with the assistance of Ann Brock and Shelly Matthews, 153–95. New York: Crossroad, 1998.

———. *The Corinthian Women Prophets: A Reconstruction through Paul's Rhetoric*. Minneapolis: Fortress, 1991.

Witherington, Ben III. *Conflict and Community in Corinth: A Socio-Rhetorical Commentary on 1 and 2 Corinthians*. Grand Rapids: Eerdmans, 1995.

www.ingramcontent.com/pod-product-compliance
Lightning Source LLC
Chambersburg PA
CBHW031432060726
47600CB00002B/13